Twayne's United States Authors Series

Sylvia E. Bowman, *Editor*

INDIANA UNIVERSITY

Bernard Wolfe

BERNARD WOLFE

By CAROLYN GEDULD

211

Twayne Publishers, Inc. :: New York

Library of Congress Catalog Card Number: 78–187612

MANUFACTURED IN THE UNITED STATES OF AMERICA

For Harry

Preface

Bernard Wolfe, one of our most remarkable and prolific living American writers, has received little critical or public attention. There has been no book-length study of his work; only one, primarily descriptive, article about him has been published; only his novel about Trotsky has been reviewed extensively; and few of his novels are easily available in libraries or bookstores. The purpose of this study, then, is to provide an introduction to a writer of considerable interest who has been quite unjustly neglected. Because of spatial limitations, it has not been possible to analyze the whole of Wolfe's published work. Regrettably, Wolfe's very fine body of short pieces and stories, including those collected in *Move Up/ Dress Up/ Drink Up/ Burn Up,* have not been discussed in this study, except fleetingly in the Selected Bibliography. In passing, though, it might be noted that the themes and characters of his short stories are much like those in his novels.

In this study, three of Wolfe's most "archetypal" novels—*Really the Blues, Limbo,* and *The Great Prince Died*—are discussed extensively as masterworks, while the remaining novels are treated in separate chapters as recapitulations of ideas Wolfe was obsessively obliged to return to again and again. The special focus of the criticism throughout this study is on Wolfe's complex psychoanalytic theory and on his indebtedness to Dr. Edmund Bergler, as these are the qualities of his work that might be particularly baffling to the uninitiated reader.

I wish to express my gratitude for the help I have received from the Institute for Sex Research at Indiana University, where I have been able to read the work Wolfe published in *Playboy, Cavalier,* and *Nugget.* My thanks go as well to Wolfe's agent, Donald Congdon; to Murray Sperber, who made invaluable suggestions; and to my husband, who originally persuaded me to read Wolfe and then offered me every encouragement while working on this project.

Bernard Wolfe has known about this study since its inception and has offered me great assistance, through correspondence and a delightful interview, for which I can only offer the admittedly favorable bias of my work in gratitude.

CAROLYN GEDULD

Contents

Chronology

1915 Bernard Wolfe born in New Haven, Connecticut, on September 28. His father, a Russian Jewish immigrant, a factory foreman; his mother, of Polish Jewish origin.

1931–1936 Enrolled as a premedical student at Yale University, where he did honors work in psychology in preparation for a career in psychiatry. After graduation in June, 1935, enrolled for a few months' additional study at Yale's Graduate Division of General Studies. During summer of 1936, taught at College of Women Trade Unionists at Bryn Mawr.

1933–1937 Became disaffected with Stalinists at Yale; began an association with Trotskyites in New Haven and New York. Wrote for Trotskyite publications, *The New International* and *The Militant*.

1937 Arrived in Mexico in January to be Trotsky's secretary and a member of his security staff. Years later, this experience inspired *The Great Prince Died.*

1937–1939 Occasionally worked in the Merchant Marines, on a "trip card" status.

1939–1940 Moved to Greenwich Village. Met Anaïs Nin and Henry Miller. Through their efforts, found employment as a writer of pornography. Wrote eleven such novels in one year, earning an average of a dollar a manuscript page.

1941 Assistant night editor for Paramount Newsreel for a few weeks.

1943–1945 Pop-science period. Frequent contributor to *Mechanix Illustrated* and *Popular Science Monthly*. Published *How to Get a Job in the Aircraft Industry* in 1943. Features Editor for *Mechanix Illustrated* from March, 1944, to November, 1944. Editor of *Mechanix Illustrated* from December, 1944, to October, 1945.

1946 *Really the Blues.*
1947– 1950, 1953 Hired as a ghost writer for Billy Rose's syndicated column "Pitching Horseshoes." Underwent analysis with Dr. Edmund Bergler.
1952 *Limbo.*
1954 *The Late Risers.*
1955– 1956 Wrote television plays produced in New York and California.
1957 *In Deep.* Wrote monthly column for *Nugget.*
1959 *The Great Prince Died.* Moved to Hollywood to do occasional work on film scripts until 1963.
1961 *The Magic of Their Singing.*
1963 *Come on Out, Daddy.*
1964 Married film actress Dolores Michaels in June.
1966– 1968 Taught a course in creative writing at University of California in Los Angeles. Wrote occasional book reviews for *Book Week* in the *New York Herald Tribune.*
1968 *Move Up/ Dress Up/ Drink Up/ Burn Up.*

Bernard Wolfe

CHAPTER 1

Who Is Bernard Wolfe?

I *The Man*

BERNARD WOLFE is the author of six novels, a biography, several television plays, and a good number of articles, short stories, and reviews. Now a man slightly past his mid-fifties, one of his most singular achievements has been to support himself for the past three decades by writing, even though his work has been largely ignored by serious critics. Between his "significant" publications, Wolfe has written pornography, edited *Mechanix Illustrated*, ghost-written Billy Rose's syndicated column, and worked on film scripts in Hollywood, the rewards of which have been to make creative periods financially possible and to purchase the deluxe Beverly Hills house and swimming pool where he and his wife presently live.

When he is in New York, Wolfe will stay and perhaps grant a luncheon interview at the Algonquin Hotel—the writers' hotel. He is a very small man with a thick, sprouting mustache, fat cigar, and a voice that grabs attention. Not inappropriately, he looks exactly like Jerry Colonna, the former radio and movie comedian famous for his loud and funny noises. For two hours straight, Wolfe talks, not the bits and pieces of conversation, but the completely developed stories of a born raconteur, about Henry Miller, Trotsky, Spain, Cuba, the television industry, boys-in-the-backroom scandal, the score, the inside story—but never quite. There's always a detail or two missing, an ace kept up the sleeve, saved, perhaps, for a bigger game.

After two hours, he stops. He's not tired. He's a trouper and a good showman who always leaves them laughing. Leaning over to a quiet friend at the table, he says, "Come up to my room for a drink." Upstairs, he will tell the *real* story, the whole mess from beginning to end, while the rest are left—now out of the charmed circle—to mull over coffee. He and his friend walk away. At the elevator, he turns and waves. In the half-light, he does not look like Jerry Colonna anymore. He looks remarkably like Stalin.

Later, Wolfe corresponds on shocking bright yellow paper. He leaves three-inch margins on each side, his words typed in a thin column down the middle of the page, full of unorthodox capitalizations and abbreviations, and a giant's signature at the bottom in brown ink. His letters come sporadically in bunches of two or three after an interval of months, and they sparkle, again, with anecdotes, the confidential inside story about Spain, Trotsky, and, more recently, women's liberation, Maoists in California, the proletarian novel. All the uniquely relevant interests, the intense obsessiveness, the wit and the charm found repeatedly in his fiction.

II *The Writer*

In general, the philosophical content of Wolfe's work represents the collective leap from Marx to Freud that characterized many of the radical intellectuals of the 1930's and early 1940's who were disillusioned by Stalinism. Wolfe's association with Trotsky was superseded a decade or so later by his involvement with the neo-Freudian theories of Dr. Edmund Bergler, the analyst of "psychic masochism." Consequently, Wolfe's early books tend to be political novels rationalized by psychoanalysis, and in particular, by the challenge to political and social systems made by Freud in *Civilization and Its Discontents.* In *Limbo* (1952), for instance, which is set in 1990, a government whose platform is passive resistance is toppled by society's "death wish." In his novel *In Deep* (1957), agents of both the CIA and the GPU (Soviet secret police) are undermined by their own "ambivalence." In *The Great Prince Died* (1959), the character representing Trotsky "allows" himself to be assassinated in answer to a "masochistic" need. In *The Magic Of Their Singing* (1961), the pre-1967 Arab-Israeli hostilities are treated as the "pseudo-aggressive" acts of psychic look-alikes.

Wolfe is probably one of the first writers to incorporate the teachings of psychoanalysis, not only into character and plot, but into theme, style, and setting—indeed into the very fabric and concept of his work. But those readers who find his Freudian "propaganda" unpalatable may be attracted instead by the often esoteric subject matters of Wolfe's books. The first, *Really the Blues* (1946), co-authored with Mezz Mezzrow, is a biography of

Mezz, a white Dixieland jazz musician who "crossed the color line." *Limbo* is a science-fiction, antiutopian novel about a people who replace their arms and legs with atomic-powered, prosthetic limbs. *The Late Risers* (1954) concerns a number of Damon Runyonesque Broadway types. *In Deep* is a thriller involving the cold war in pre-Castro Cuba. *The Great Prince Died* is Wolfe's novel about Trotsky; *The Magic of Their Singing*, the "hipsters" in Greenwich Village; *Come on Out, Daddy* (1963), the film industry.

Wolfe has also had two books ghost-written for him (by Raymond Rosenthal) in the 1940's, when he was the editor of *Mechanix Illustrated*. The first of these, *Plastics, What Everyone Should Know* (1945), is a part of a series which popularized various branches of technology. *Hypnotism Comes of Age, Its Progress from Mesmer to Psychoanalysis* (1948), written while Wolfe was drafting *Limbo*, concerns the history of hypnotism as "a tool of modern medicine." In the same period, Wolfe wrote on commission *How to Get a Job in the Aircraft Industry* (1943): as the title suggests, this soft-cover publication gives information about opportunities in airplane factories.

III *The Prototypic Novel*

These "scientific" writings, however, have had no direct influence on Wolfe's "serious" books. The prototypic Wolfean plot, by contrast, is set in a highly charged political climate in which the opponents (East-West, black-white, "hip"-orthodox) tend secretly to resemble each other. Into this atmosphere is thrown a hero who has the special ability to objectify and verbalize both his own problems and those of the society which reflects them. Frequently, the hero's parents participate in a reversal of the traditional parental roles of mother as the weaker and father as the stronger; and, while living with them, the hero experiences a childhood trauma which causes his "neurosis." As an adult, the hero is a "psychic masochist" and often a writer whose "joke book" is taken seriously by the society that reads it. Typically, the hero chooses a heroine noted for some spectacular sort of frigidity (which Wolfe interprets as the inability to achieve vaginal orgasm). During the narrative, both the hero and heroine are "cured"; and the hero, always a rebel (for "masochistic" reasons), therapeutically attacks the society he has often helped create. In the end, the hero and heroine leave society for a primitive island where they live frugally, work hard, and marry.

The form most characteristic of Wolfe's work is the deliberate "parody" of popular literary genres, such as science fiction, the Damon Runyon-type story, the thriller, the Hollywood novel. Fundamentally, Wolfe's kind of "parody" encompasses fictionalized literary criticism: he analyzes a specific form (the "thriller," for example), draws conclusions (the "private eye" really chases another image of himself), and then writes his "parody" (*In Deep,* in which the "private eye" is the "mirror image" of the villain). Nevertheless, despite Wolfe's intellectualization of his "parodies," one of memorable things about his novels is their great wit. The "belly laugh" coupled with the attack on contemporary society (and contemporary literature) are the distinctive hallmarks of Wolfe's work.

Yet, Wolfe's first work, *Really the Blues,* is in many ways atypical (perhaps because it was co-authored). The dichotomy between the biography and the "prototypic" novels is one that Wolfe has tried to resolve within his fiction, a subject discussed in subsequent pages.

CHAPTER 2

Really the Blues

I *Wolfe's First Book*

WITH the publication in 1946 of *Really the Blues,* co-authored by Bernard Wolfe and Mezz Mezzrow, American black literature received one of its most offbeat contributions. The book is a biography of Mezz, a white Jewish boy who "joins" the black race and adopts their music, their language, and their attitudes toward whites. Six years earlier, by contrast, Richard Wright's *Native Son* had drawn critical attention to the chronicle of a black man as told from a black point of view. And in the same decade, Faulkner's *Intruder in the Dust* continued the tradition of treating blacks as the underside of the white southern conscience. *Really the Blues* stands somewhere between and slightly beyond these other two books, not only because of the hero's equivocal racial status, but because of the book's equal fascination with classical jazz and drugs. The difficulty of finding a literary context for the work increases with its flouting of genre as well as of race: biography and fiction (or, at least, fictive techniques) are combined, as Mezz tells his "story," and often it is impossible to distinguish truth from fantasy in the jazzman's recall. There is, moreover, a good deal of technical documentation of the process of performing jazz, a point not missed by the many booksellers who stock copies in their shops' "music" sections.

Wolfe's first book, typically for him, is a literary teaser: it provokes delicate critical problems of definition, not the least of which involves a study of *Really the Blues* as a collaborative effort. In the last few paragraphs of the book, which is narrated throughout from Mezz's point of view, Wolfe makes a brief appearance as a character. Mezz is playing in a jam session, "when in wanders this young white fellow who tells me he don't know much about music, he's a writer, but he likes my records fine—they're a kind of jazz you don't get much anymore. He's figuring on doing some kind of magazine article about me and what do I think of the idea?"(333). Mezz responds by talking about himself for a couple of years, while Wolfe, his "literary pal," listens and writes (presumably with greater caution than would the annotators of the journal of *Limbo*'s hero). The finished manuscript is book-length, and its publication as a collective work emphasizes and heightens a spirit which pervades its narrative, themes, and style.

II Really the Blues: *Plot*

The biography of Mezz Mezzrow, as it is developed in *Really the Blues,* is a significant historical and sociological document about America from the turn of the century until the eve of World War II. The book is, indeed, as Mezz puts it, "a chunk of Americana" about which little can be obtained from standard sources, for it includes a history of classical jazz from its birth in New Orleans to the death of "hot" jazz in the early 1940's; an account of race relations in northern ghettos and jails; and a view of the underworld during Prohibition, with frequent glimpses of such notorious figures as Al Capone and his rivals, the Purple Gang. Furthermore, Mezz's life is recounted against historical backdrops which could have been witnessed only from the streets, as, for instance, the Chicago race riot of 1919 and the St. Valentine's Day Massacre.

The narrative bulk of the book concerns the adventures of Mezz from his birth in 1899 until his meeting with Wolfe in the mid-1940's. Milton Mezzrow, the son of Jewish immigrant parents, has been reared on the streets of Chicago where he falls under the tutelage of minor thugs and gangsters. Even at this stage, however, he instinctively searches for a mode of expression which would take him beyond the poolroom. Ironically, his revelation occurs in Pontiac, a reformatory, where he first befriends blacks and learns to play the flute, the piccolo, and the saxophone for the prison band. At the same time, he witnesses a small-scale race riot in Pontiac, which he takes as a personal assault: "I felt so close to those Negroes, it was just like I'd seen a gang attack on my own family" (16). Shortly after his release from Pontiac, Mezz and his friends travel to Missouri, where, because of their dark and dirt-covered complexions, they are called "niggers." "We were Jews, but in Cape Girardeau they had told us we were Negroes. Now, all of sudden, I realized I agreed with them" (18). From this point on, Mezz identifies wholly with the black race. He learns their music, their language, and their philosophy; and he eventually lives exclusively in black ghettos.

Mezz is to "do time" on two occasions after Pontiac before accepting his first job in a jazz band. Meanwhile, he discovers New Orleans jazz on Chicago's South Side and is immediately converted. When he hears the New Orleans Rhythm Kings, however, he realizes that even a white man can play black music, and he decides to become a musician. The period between 1923 and 1928 proves to be one of the most creative periods of his career. While continually striving to approach the New Orleans sound, he works for Al Capone in such speakeasies as the Arrowhead Inn and the Roadside Home. He soon acquires a working knowledge of the brutality of gangsterdom: the exploitation of prostitutes, the terrorization of the speakeasy management, and the bodies found in ditches.

In 1924, Mezz begins to smoke marihuana. At the same time, he meets Bix Beiderbecke, who would later be "corrupted" by the music of Debussy, Ravel, and Stravinsky. His friendship with Bix leads to a recognition of the differences between the jazz that the white man plays and the far more "solid" music of the New Orleans school. Two years later, Mezz joins the Austin High Gang, a group of white boys who initiate the Chicago style of jazz, which creeps further and further away from the black idiom. Eventually, Mezz and the Chicagoans drift apart, the latter emigrating to New York and the big commercial bands. Mezz becomes the "forgottenest man in town," unable to find a job or to resolve the conflict between black and white jazz.

During the early 1930's, Mezz visits Harlem and Paris, and he suffers a breakdown in health and spirit. In France, a meeting with Hugh Panassié, an enthusiastic jazz scholar, serves as a partial cure for Mezz. Returned to the United States, he initiates the Louis Armstrong craze in Harlem, where he is known as "the Link Between the Races." He also introduces the New York blacks to the "mezzerole," a type of marihuana which is purer than anything else sold in Harlem at the time. But in spite of his popularity and his friendship with Armstrong, circumstances militate against Mezz and perpetuate his second decline. His only defense against his unwanted "whiteness" is to make music, but he can only play in the style of the black musicians; and, because there are no racially mixed bands in existence at that time, he is forced to give up his musical career. While supporting himself by pushing "mezzeroles," Mezz begins to smoke opium. Soon he is "hooked" and spends the next five years in a coal cellar with Mick and Mackey, two fellow addicts.

Not until 1935 does Mezz gain an incentive for "kicking" his habit. At this time the mixed-band idea becomes a distant possibility when Louis Armstrong, who knows nothing about his friend's addiction, asks Mezz to be his musical director. Realizing the importance of Louis' gesture in terms of both the racial and the musical situation, he prepares himself for a final battle between his physical and his spiritual needs. The climax of the book occurs after the ordeal, when Mezz is virtually reborn. He must relearn the most basic muscular actions, like walking and feeding himself, as well as the simplest of human relationships. His new health leads to additional changes: he obtains a friendly divorce from his white wife and moves permanently to Harlem, where he meets and marries a black woman; he begins to make music again; eventually, he leads the first all-star mixed band on Broadway in a performance which, nevertheless, is closed after only a few days.

The final phase of Mezz's rebirth occurs, again, in jail; for, sentenced to a term on Riker's Island for possession of marihuana, which is by then illegal, he "passes" for black and is permitted to join the black block. Soon after, he is transferred to Harts Island, a prison with an emphasis on rehabilitation. There he is able to devote himself to music without the distractions of selling "mezzeroles" or fighting jim crow regulations. Shortly before he is due to leave the jail, he discovers the key to New Orleans jazz, a problem which has been vexing him since he first heard black jazz on the South Side of Chicago. From this point on, Mezz achieves musical maturity and is seldom without a job. He forms a recording company, King Jazz, Inc.; rears a family in Harlem; and finally finds a "literary" friend in Wolfe.

III Really the Blues: *Form*

Mezz's experiences do not relate to each other in a clearly causal chain of events, as might be suggested by the summary. Rather, they evolve from numerous, loosely connected anecdotes, some no more than a paragraph or two long, "each one adding another brick to the simple and sturdy structure" (340), a description applying equally both to jazz and to this book. There are unforgettable accounts, for instance, of Louis Armstrong's performing with a mangled lip, of Bessie Smith's death, of the black doctor who saved Hugh Panassié's life, of Mezz's "rescue" of a prostitute from the Chicago syndicate, and of his feigning tuberculosis in order to avoid hard labor in jail.

These anecdotes act upon the main theme and story much as improvisations do upon the melodic line of New Orleans jazz. The reader is subtly urged to ignore the larger issues in favor of an easy appreciation of the book's seemingly "spontaneous" nature, a mood invoked partially by the work's loose construction. In effect, *Really the Blues* strives to imitate its subject: the jazz idiom itself. The prose and the structure attempt to reach beyond language to something more basic and more communicable—music. In the book's most experimental chapter, a section written in "jive" (a "language" supposedly spoken by blacks and jazzmen), the prose is quite unintelligible for the ordinary reader without consultation with the glossary and the "translation" appended to the narrative. Also, there are essays in an additional appendix on the differences between New Orleans jazz and its derivatives and on "Panassié recordings," which serve to "explain" some of the technogical material infused in the language and narrative. The reader unacquainted with the jazz idiom needs these aids to understand a narrative which makes a few concessions to the uninitiated.

Yet, the tremendous vitality of jive in *Really the Blues* is enough to carry the reader along who is not familiar with classical jazz and with the many notable musicians, gangsters, and speakeasies mentioned. (Again, there is an analogy with jazz, whose spirit often excited listeners who did not understand the intricacies of the performance.) The language of the book borrows freely, not only from jive, but also from the lyrics of blues and jazz songs. The title, for instance, is taken from one of Mezz's recordings; and the chapter headings are from such classic songs as Bessie Smith's "A Nothin' But a Child" and Louis Armstrong's "Got the Heebies, Got the Jeebies." The latent power of these lyrics—as well as of jive, of jazz, and of the ancedotes in the book—is found, according to Mezz, in the "bellylaugh" buried in the blacks' racial character.

The popularity of Wolfe's first book, which was still in print twenty years after its original publication in 1946, probably can be understood in the 1970's as that form of oblique racism which used to manifest itself in the literary quest for "frontiers." There is a touch of James Fenimore Cooper, not only in the open yearning for black ("savage") pleasure, but also in the book's settings: the largely "unexplored" no-man's-lands of ghettos, jails, poolrooms, and the "untouched" territories of marihuana, hard drugs, and syndicated crime. (In later novels, Wolfe retained an interest in such contemporary "frontiers" as Hollywood, Mexico, Cuba, as well as in that temporal "frontier," the future.) Mezz, like so many of Wolfe's heroes, is something of an explorer whose recorded adventures allow society a glimpse of a less "civilized" (from a middle-class perspective) culture—that of Negroes, junkies, and jazzmen—from a safe distance. And, typically for its premilitant era, if such a culture is used to attack the values of bourgeois America, the reader is apt to be equally fascinated by the lure of the forbidden.

In *Really the Blues*, the "forbidden" pleasures tabooed by the repressive nature of white society are rediscovered in the ghetto, where the black man as "Noble Savage" is engaged, fundamentally, in a re-enactment of the Dionysiac myth. The substrata of ritual, Dionysian among the blacks and Apollonian among the whites, is the esthetic binding that holds together the seemingly anarchic narrative of the book. In fact, in the appendix of his second book, *Limbo*, Wolfe admits being influenced both by the description of Apollonian and Dionysian societies in Ruth Benedict's anthropological work *Patterns of Culture* and by Nietzsche's discussion of Dionysus in *The Birth of Tragedy from the Spirit of Music*, "the only book I know which says something about bebop" (436). *Really the Blues* represents a careful working out, indeed an Americanization, of the Greek myth, which has equivalents in this country's mythic "frontier." Although Wolfe later rejected the "Noble Savage" as well as the Dionysiac individual, he characteristically uses in his first book an archetypal situation to explain a contemporary "neurosis."

IV *Dionysus and the Jazzman*

The hints in later works that Wolfe gives about the mythic elements in *Really the Blues* are supplemented by internal evidence in the book of a special attention to form, which stands behind the jazzman's "spontaneous" way of life. There are distinctly religious overtones—pagan to be sure—in Mezz's "metaphysical" use of marihuana, in the "ecstasies" associated with jazz, in physical "ordeals," and in the "rebirth" of the jazzmen and his subsequent reaffirmation of life. Moreover, there is a priestly relationship between Mezz and his colleagues; after learning the rudiments of jazz from the original New Orleans "gods," he "enlightens" the black and white musicians in the North, admonishing those heretics who deviate from the "purity" of authentic Dixieland. But it is the spirit of excess within the jazzman's "religion"—the frequent inability, for instance, to separate enthusiasm from mania during performances—that suggests the metaphoric worship of Dionysus. The similarities between the Greek myth and that of the American bohemia during and after Prohibition are clearly those appealing to the most primitive tendencies of instinctual man.

Dionysus, whose name means "twice born," was a demigod, the son of an earth woman, Semele, and of Zeus. Soon after the child was born, Hera, the wife of Zeus, ordered the dismemberment of Dionysus, but he was resurrected by his grandmother, Rhea. To save his son, Zeus then hid him in the women's quarters, where he grew to manhood and invented wine. Eventually, however, Hera discovered his whereabouts and tortured him with a madness that compelled him to wander throughout Asia, where his followers were the satyrs and maenads who craved his wine. Before being cured again by Rhea, Dionysus and his maddened army brutally slaughtered all who stood in their way. But following his return to sanity, he began seeking converts to his wine cult in Europe and punishing those who refused to honor him, significantly, with an inflicted madness that forced his enemies to tear their own children to pieces and often to devour them as well. The worshipers of Dionysus, on the other hand, were touched by an ecstasy during which they dismembered and devoured animals. (This was perhaps a symbolic devouring of Dionysus himself, who was traditionally supposed to assume the likenesses of the animals involved.) After many years, the god-man ascended to heaven, where he sat at the right hand of Zeus.

While the myth tends to emphasize the negative characteristics of Dionysus—his "madness," the dismemberment and cannibalism associated with his cult, his wanderlust—Euripides' *The Bacchae* describes a more attractive figure, a god of the oppressed, to whom he brings the simple, physical pleasures of food, wine, and general intoxication.

Mezz's life parallels that of Dionysus in many respects. The jazzman is also confined in his youth, in jail, where he identifies, not with a woman, but with his opposite number in another form —the black man. There he falls under the influence of the music which is called "madness" by those who do not like it; and, upon his release from prison, he "wanders," like a missionary, from Chicago to Paris seeking converts. While he does not invent marihuana—the "wine" of the jazz cultist—he introduces "mezzeroles," a superior type of marihuana, to Harlem, thereby achieving fame throughout the ghetto as the "Reefer King." But before his "ascension to Heaven"—the happiness described in the last pages of *Really the Blues*—Mezz undergoes a physical and psychological "dismemberment" during the five years of his addiction to opium; and during his subsequent cure, he is almost literally "torn limb from limb." Like Dionysus, however, Mezz is torn apart in order to be reborn, after which he can appreciate the simple pleasures associated with his mythic predecessor.

His "converts," as much intoxicated by New Orleans jazz as by marihuana, participate in the orgiastic frenzy of the ancient satyrs and maenads. During one of Mezz's performances, he describes a typical enthusiast, who "was throwing herself around like a snake with the hives. . . . Her eyes almost jumped out of their sockets and the cords of her neck stood out stiff and hard like ropes. What she was doing with the rest of her anatomy isn't discussed in mixed company" (75). After her frantic dance, "she fell to the floor like a hunk of putty and lay in a heap, quivering and making those funny noises way down in her throat" (76). This obviously sexual release is a short step away in intensity from the Dionysian extreme in which orgasm is accompanied by physical dismemberment.

The one striking omission of a Dionysian counterpart in *Really the Blues* is that of the matriarchal forces: the murderous goddess, Hera, and her opposite, the beneficent Rhea. On a conscious level, at least, women are strangely excluded from Mezz's world. The names of his wives are mentioned only in passing, and as characters they barely exist at all. Here the myth of Dionysus is subtly superseded by our own mythic "frontier," in which the legendary

Natty Bumpos forfeit domestic ties for a "safer," primarily nonsexual involvement with their masculine savage friends. (In his second work, Wolfe treats such isolationism by men as an infantile attempt to escape from the fantasized "dangerous" mothers who might indeed attempt to "dismember" their sons.) Mezz is undeniably closer to Louis Armstrong and Hugh Panassié than to his wives.

But in *Really the Blues* the general estrangement from women is rationalized by the musicians, who consider any involvement with a woman as "tangent" to their main function—making music. Even for the white man, sexuality appears to be too close to naked aggression to gratify him. Characteristically, white sexuality is associated with gangsterism, brutality, jealousy, and a lack of any redeeming affection. This situation is not unconnected with the treatment of the typical white woman in *Really the Blues* as a prostitute. Because Mezz has a safely Platonic relationship with the "chicks" in the "cathouses," he is sensitive to the drudgery, debt, disease, and syndicate terrorization that pass for easy sexuality. And the white stripper, speakeasy entertainer, and "gun moll" are equally unappealing to the jazzman and his friends.

The black woman, by contrast, is inherently exciting, because—according to Mezz—her sexuality is not contaminated by the economic considerations that taint the white "culture of masturbators." However, the black woman is attractive precisely because her body is de-emphasized: "all she needs are healthy vocal cords and a soul, not a chassis with the seven-years-itch" (27). The Dionysiac orgy is projected in the black woman as an attempt to surpass the physical limits of the body (which is another form of "dismembering")—perhaps because, Mezz believes, the menace of a Hera can only thus be contained. At the same time, as Mezz is quick to point out, the black man is not afflicted with the white man's jealousy: if his woman is unfaithful, or even if she prostitutes herself, his "love" for her is unchanged. It is the simple and natural force that Mezz calls "clean," again a reminder of the chaste relationships characteristic of the early frontier of American literature.

At the root of *Really the Blues,* then, lies a compromise between the archetypal "frontier" and the mythic Dionysiac cult. One can, according to the jazzman, avoid the tragic "dismemberment" of white society—where Heras are all-powerful—both by "escaping" to an "untouched" territory, perhaps a black ghetto, and by participating in therapeutic emotional and physical excesses which are, however, neither sexual nor aggressive. If the Greek orgies involved an uncontrolled eruption of the id, which released the murderer as well as the reveler in man, Mezz's cult instead activates a purified Eros, while suppressing Thanatos completely. This residue of ecstasy is used to answer Freud's argument in *Civilization and Its Discontents,* in which it is postulated that society is inimical to the instinctual happiness of man. The biography of Mezz contains the possibility, within the outer bounds of contemporary civilization, of experiencing the purely physical joy, the anti-intellectual intoxication, the springtime radiance and energy found previously only in the barbaric wine cult.

The hypothesis behind this possibility is that man—if he can shield himself from many of the corruptions of modern society—is both happy and good willed in his natural state. And although Wolfe fiercely rejects Rousseau's view of human nature in all of his later novels, the central problem of his work remains: how can man cope with his aggressions under the terrible pressures of mid-twentieth-century life? In the book about jazz, Wolfe suggests that man's destructive instincts can be absorbed, specifically, by an "authentic" musical creativity which is cathartic for performer and audience alike. There is, moreover, a quality about "untainted" art alone—that is, art unmotivated by commercial or political interests—that channels the aggressions into a creative ecstasy.

For the premilitant blacks in *Really the Blues,* the special outlets for the mildly aggressive remnants not directly sublimated in their music are the "Preaching Blues," an improvised reproach in the form of a song directed at misguided colleagues, and "Cutting Contests," good-natured competitions between blacks with similar skills.

Those who cannot transform their aggressions into Dionysiac ecstasy through marihuana, jazz, or "contests," receive the full wrath of the "god" they do not honor. White Americans are punished with "madness" and destruction—although, in Wolfe's updated version of the myth, the "god" is within them, and their "punishment" is self-inflicted. Anticipating the psychoanalytic theory of "psychic masochism" which would heavily influence *Limbo,* Mezz says that "people very seldom get themselves messed up unless they have been asking for it in some way, no matter how much of an innocent victim they look like from the outside" (242). Although a more ancient people might have been literally compelled to dismember their children by the fury of Dionysus, the contemporaries of Mezz are more likely to be torn apart by their own misdirected aggressions.

When Mezz "pushes" marihuana, for instance, instead of playing jazz, his subsequent addiction to opium is seen as inevitable. The thin line between self-destruction and ecstasy is crossed when one "goes tangent"—allows destructive impulses to flow in noncreative (or nonmusical) directions. This danger is realized most dramatically in the literal dismemberment of characters in Wolfe's later novels. In *Limbo,* men voluntarily submit to the amputation of their limbs; in *Come on Out, Daddy,* maddened fans try to "tear apart" movie star Anson Luddy; in *The Great Prince Died,* the theme of the parent who kills the child he cannot recognize becomes explicit. In *Really the Blues,* however, it is an entire civilization that approaches a virtual Armageddon under Al Capone's trigger-happy influence.

In general, however, the ecstasy associated with Dionysus remains the special property of the blacks, although a white man can achieve it through "hard study" and, presumably, relinquishment of wealth and comfort for the less materialistic embellishments of the ghetto-frontier. The black man's "sensitivity and plain human respect," Mezz explains, are the gifts of his history of oppression: "The Negro never had anything before and never expects anything after, so when the blues get him he comes out smiling and without any evil feeling" (14). The white man is oppressed only by his own puritanical background—he expects a substantial reward for good works. By the 1920's, however, the good worker has become the "good" racketeer, and the reward is strictly monetary. Moreover, the white man is, without reason, a neurotic and "spoiled child" who "has the idea that because he feels bad somebody's done him wrong, and he means to take it out on somebody." But the black man does not have to distort reality so (perhaps because somebody really *has* done him wrong); consequently, his sense of injustice does not prevent him from "loving" his fellow men. Thus, whenever Mezz is in trouble, a black, often a stranger, makes him "feel good." His frequent depression is eased by the blacks' good-spirited ways: their gentle laughter, the joy of their music, their intuitive sympathy, their kindly words, and their willingness to share marihuana.

The intoxicant, which stands in the same relationship to the blacks and jazzmen as wine did for the worshipers of Dionysus, is a vehicle for ecstasy because, like Dixieland, it absorbs aggressions. Marihuana is, for that reason, compared favorably in *Really the Blues* with the destructive effects of liquor and such hard drugs as opium, which seem to excite rather than suppress the aggressive instincts. Within and around its narrative anecdotes, Wolfe's first book constantly pleads for the legalization of marihuana, a theme continued in *Limbo,* where the "masochistic" citizens of the future choose between the officially approved sedative, "Rotabunga," and the prohibited intoxicant, "Ganja." Mezz eloquently tries to argue against the "arbitrary" illegality of possession of marihuana by relating his personal experiences as a smoker of many years, pointing out, for instance, that "grass" is not addictive. Even his activities as a pusher are "justified" because he claims not to have dealings with any novices or minors and because his merchandise is the purest to be found at the time. But, beyond such rationalizations, marihuana is a part of the central mythic and religious experience in *Really the Blues:* it puts the user directly in touch with the life force itself.

The Dionysian myth in Wolfe's first book anticipates the new consciousness of the counterculture of the 1970's, in which drugs, rock music, and rural communes both literally reopen the classic "frontier" of American Western literature as well as the "frontier" of the streets, in Wolfe's special sense of the word. On the other hand, in associating the "frontier" with freedom from restraint, *Really the Blues* overlooks the oppression of Indians and the enslavement of blacks that we now recognize as the soft underbelly of early American settlement.

But in 1946, Wolfe visualized the "frontier" merely as a figurative place of archetypal freedom, untouched by the strictures of society and by domesticity. The sheer anarchy of the "frontier," where untamed man grappled with untamed nature is, by definition, Dionysian. In the absence of the Wild West, it is only in the premilitant ghetto that the wandering white man may have a "savage" for a friend, while physical ordeals and even an internally provoked "dismemberment" threaten. In *Really the Blues,* Mezz predicts that, when the white American can again respect his dark brother, when the two "dismembered" halves can again be reunited, the ecstasy and innocence of the "frontier" will be a part of the American mainland. The gifts of Dionysus are still offered to the "twice-born" man.

V *Nietzsche and Dionysus*

Wolfe's concept of Mezz's life as a modern equivalent of Dionysus' is tempered by Nietzsche's special interpretation of the myth in *The Birth of Tragedy from the Spirit of Music.* From that book, Wolfe developed his ideas about the Dionysian spirit of jazz, the contrast between jive and language, and the double meaning of dismemberment. In *The Birth of Tragedy,* Nietzsche suggests that the ancient world was divided between the worship of Apollo, the god representing "appearance," and Dionysus, the god of "truth." This dualism was formally recognized by the late period of Greek history, when Apollo's student, Socrates—who was the champion of intellectual rationalization—clashed with those who still followed Dionysus, the representative of "premordial truth." (In modern times, these still unreconciled polarities are variously called "Existence" and "Essence," "Ego" and "Id," "Head" and "Heart.") According to Nietzsche, the Apollonian and Dionysian attitudes were voiced through different vehicles of expression; Socrates verbalized his philosophy through *words,* while those who preferred Dionysus invented the "universal language" —music.

The antithesis of words and music in *Really the Blues* is still found to be viable in twentieth-century America. For the Apollonian culture of the white man, however, language and the intellectual process have reached their most monstrous and self-limiting forms, producing rationalized violence, a racial hierarchy, and various forms of oppression. Black music, on the other hand, is the ultimate expression of Dionysian freedom. A democratic force, it appeals to wealthy and indigent alike, and it finds enthusiasts among Europeans and Asians as well as among Americans. The universal intoxicant at the root of jazz is said, by Mezz, to be found in its most primitive form, the Blues. Originally, the blacks on work gangs cheered themselves by singing; and, while their songs referred to their oppression, they also expressed an unsuppressed joy that was Dionysian in spirit. When the Blues were later transformed into New Orleans jazz as blacks migrated to the cities, where they were relatively better off, the original joy developed into the current of laughter basic to the essence of Dixieland. From its inception, jazz has contained a strong affirmation of life. It is an expression of the "rebel instincts" which impel man to cling stubbornly to life in spite of its tragedy.

The special freedom associated with jazz (in distinction to other forms of music) is best indicated by the spontaneous character of performances, which are, as a rule, improvised. In *Really the Blues*, few of the jazzmen go to music school or receive any formal training; they learn to play, as it were, through instinct and sheer passion. Once their skill is perfected, the musicians prefer a jam session—"a musical get-together in which all the playing is collectively improvised"; but, even when they perform before an audience, they work through head arrangements—"a musical arrangement by ear, without written music." Their antipathy for sheet music and for composition is symptomatic of the anti-intellectual and antirational attitudes which Nietzsche called Dionysian. In fact, Mezz's friendship with Bix Beiderbecke is terminated precisely because of the latter's interest in the "composed," indeed "Apollonian," music of Ravel and Stravinsky. Significantly, Mezz notes the early deaths of Bix and other jazzmen who "go tangent" musically.

Even the poet, according to Nietzsche, senses the superiority of music and sometimes tries to imitate it through language, most successfully through folk poetry. In *Really the Blues*, the experiments with jive—the folk poetry of the blacks—similarily attempt to go beyond the limitations of prose. The lyrics of jazz, for instance, as sung by such artists as Bessie Smith, are linguistic distortions—the elongated vowels and dropped consonants are concessions to the more forceful melodic line of the blues. But with the birth of Louis Armstrong's "Vo-do-de-o" school of lyrics, the function of language in jazz clearly becomes superfluous, drawing jazzmen closer to a purely musical statement.

Jive, moreover, is the folk poetry which is second only to the "Vo-do-de-o" lyrics in its break down of the Apollonian mode of expression. Possibly the strongest section of *Really the Blues* contains a long essay on the nature of jive, which is indebted in part to such jive scholars as Dave Burlet and Earl Conrad and which is preceded by a chapter written entirely in ghetto "language." Like all folk poetry, Mezz insists, it is essential for jive to be vocalized rather than perpetuated in written form.

In *Really the Blues*, this need for vocalization is acknowledged. Mezz "tells his story" directly, even conversationally, often interrupting his anecdotes to answer the unvoiced questions the reader presumably would ask, as if the book were really a "live" interview rather than a literary experience. The assumption of a personal contact between subject and audience is present even in the opening sentences of the book: "Music school? Are you kidding? I learned to play the sax in Pontiac Reformatory" (3).

In a sense, *Really the Blues* becomes one of Marshall McLuhan's "hot media" which forces the reader to participate in the dialogue and, eventually, to "understand" a language based on nonsense words. The success of the method can be determined by those readers who intuitively guess, without consulting the glossary, that the last lines of the work—"This is the book. If it got in you mouth, don't fault me" (335)—mean "If it repelled you, don't blame me." Through an acceptance of the "dismemberment" of the white man's language, the reader is subtly encouraged to negate the Apollonian "ritual" that he intended to observe by the very act of deciding to read a book.

For Mezz's blacks, however, jive represents an *active* protest against the white man's oppression. Noting that the "smooth talkers" in white society are successful, at least monetarily, the black man mocks both the "fraud of language" and the fraudulent success he himself cannot aspire to. Jive, Mezz believes, partakes in the laughter underlying jazz and the blues, because it connotes "a fine sense of the ridiculous that had behind it some solid social criticism" (228). The humor in jive, however, has its aggressive counterpart which is meant to mangle the white man's language, symbolically tearing the oppressors "from limb to limb." As a means of resistance, the Dionysian function of jive, like jazz, is to gain the freedom anticipated by Nietzsche, in which "the slave emerges as a freeman; all the rigid, hostile walls which either necessity or despotism has erected between man are shattered." [1]

Nietzsche's idea of freedom evolved from his concept of God as a creative artist and of the act of creation as the means by which man can merge with "the primal architect of the cosmos." The "genius" who can through creation "know something of the eternal essence of art" becomes "at once subject and object, poet, actor, and audience." [2] While Nietzsche's notion of the "genius" approaches his later idea of the "Superman," Wolfe—who is a proletarian writer at heart—adapts the theory for his own purposes by substituting the "bottom-dog" for "the genius." The black musician who "creates" jazz becomes, like God, a composer, performer, arranger, and spectator and he is, in this special sense, free. It is not without significance that the merger of man and God involves the forgetting—or, again, "dismemberment"—of self, and thus, the Dionysiac ecstasy ultimately coincides with Dionysiac suffering; both are a means of denying the prison of one's skin, the separation of "self" from "other."

If Mezz does not quite realize that the underside of pain is pleasure, a theme dramatized most explicitly in *Limbo,* his life is nevertheless a continual, almost ritualistic, negation of self, as he retreats from and then approaches the Dionysian extreme. In his youth, he alienates himself from his traditional past by rejecting his race, religion, and family. He proceeds to dissociate himself from society by becoming involved with gangsters and eventually serving several sentences in jail. During his years as an addict, furthermore, he loses touch with fundamental reality; and, during his cure, he is physically "torn apart." If he becomes in the end a new man whose new race is officially recognized by the draft board, his rebirth is simply the first step toward his achievement of the ultimate release from existence alluded to in his last testament: "When I wash away, just take my body and shove it in one of them blast furnaces, and when I'm melted down good, scrape out the dust and mix it up with some shellac and press it into a record" (333). In this deceptively humble vision, the performer of music succeeds in reaching that cosmic nirvana where music and musician are inseparable; where, in other words, essence outlives existence and truth endures without appearance.

The "authentic" New Orleans jazzmen in *Really the Blues* share this sense of universal oneness and the denial of individual importance by refusing to give solo performances. Their style is based instead on the principle of "collective improvisation" in which the musicians merge their talents. Through the "dismemberment" of the individuals in the group, an "inner life" is released which spontaneously creates good music. Presumably, the same method can apply, in theory, to the writing of a book, and thus the co-authorship of Mezzrow and Wolfe can, in this sense, be viewed as an effort to merge the writer with his subject (and with them, through the stylistic subtleties already discussed, the reader).

VI *The Myth and Reality*

Ironically, this very tendency to "package," to find a secret merger or connection between dissimilar things and people, is most decisively attacked in all of Wolfe's later work. Even before the publication of *Limbo,* articles written by Wolfe suggest that the ideas put forth in *Really the Blues* are misleading at best. Nevertheless, at least two elements in the biography of Mezz appear frequently, although in changed forms, in subsequent novels. The "bellylaugh" fundamental to Wolfe's conception of both the blacks' personality and the Dionysian spirit becomes the "joke" around which many later novels are structured. And the discussion of "aggression," healthy and unhealthy, preoccupies the heroes of Wolfe, from Martine in *Limbo* to Gordon in *Come on Out, Daddy.*

But for the student of Wolfe, *Really the Blues* is notable because he has not, to date, written another book like it. The novels written after 1946 are clearly the products of a rationalist whose thoroughly professional talents seldom allow the linguistic experimentation, the anarchic structure, the suppression of individuality (and consequently, character), and the lack of "scientific" verification to jeopardize highly complex and intricately motivated themes.

Really the Blues also contains what is thus far Wolfe's only viable use of a Classical substructure. In later work, his concern is rather to *destroy* mythic and stereotyped elements which are often imposed upon a people from the outside, a view that appropriately applies to his early biography of Mezz. Hence, an article entitled "Uncle Remus and the Malevolent Rabbit" *Commentary* (July, 1949), an extract from an unpublished manuscript on the black and be-bop cultures, suggests that the white man, who really knows nothing about the black, *invents* "a negative print of his own uneasy self: 'happy-go-lucky,' socializing, orally expressive, unashamedly exhibitionistic, free from self-pity even in his situation of concentrated pain" (40).

This falsified "Negro," Wolfe argues, is the white man's secret ego ideal, and his desire to emulate him must be camouflaged by a conscious attitude of oppression, hatred, or intolerance. In this sense, *Really the Blues* may have been a popular book precisely because it gives the white man the myth he wanted: the *un*menacing black who is "ecstatic" rather than violent; a white man who could, in a world where all things are possible, "cross the color line" without superego objections; frequent endorsement of less provocative taboos—drugs, crime, bohemia; and a "frontier" where innocence and freedom still exist. The attractive Dionysian myth in *Really the Blues* overtakes the no doubt bleaker reality: that black discontent has not been appeased by music or by marihuana. That was rather the hope of a white society before it learned to fear the consequences of ghetto uprisings in the 1960's. For Wolfe, a greater sensitivity to the American character—black as well as white—would emerge in *Limbo*.

CHAPTER 3

Limbo

I *Beyond* Really the Blues

THREE years after the publication of Orwell's *1984*, an equally impressive, although totally different, antiutopian novel appeared in its shadow. *Limbo*—or *Limbo 90*, as its abridged form is called in England—is Bernard Wolfe's first novel. It is, moreover, the most ambitious of Wolfe's works to date; a source study alone would probably involve a background reading of more than fifty related books. But beyond its scope and brilliance, *Limbo* can be viewed as the dividing line between the early Wolfe—the co-author of one obliquely racist biography, *Really the Blues;* two truly significant essays on Black culture; and several "scientific" and political articles and books which must be regarded as trivia—and the Wolfe who has been writing since 1952. *Limbo* is the genesis, not only of all the later novels in regard to theme and style, but also of Wolfe's abandonment of journalism for a career as a writer of fiction.

The differences between *Limbo* and *Really the Blues* can partially be accounted for by the six-year gap between their publications; during these years Wolfe fell under the influence of the works of psychoanalyst Edmund Bergler. Wolfe's enthusiasm for Bergler's theories was incompatible with Mezz Mezzrow's belief in fellowship, the annihilation of the individual in communal spirit, and the Dionysian way of life. Rather, the novels written after *Really the Blues* recognize man as an ambivalent animal, seeking pain in the name of pleasure, as much Apollonian as Dionysian. *Limbo,* in fact, not only attacks the Dionysian attitude as a vehicle for the death wish but even, in passing, New Orleans jazz. The "time-saddled" society of the future revives classical jazz in a pretense of opposition to the technology it secretly loves; and, appropriately, Dixieland is now interpreted as a mere *flirtation* "with the idea of disrupting schedule and smashing the metronome—a toying, a nihilistic charade, but never a complete breakthrough" (99-100). The very joy associated with jazz is thought of as sham, as one of the "traps of the community" (100).

As we have noted, Wolfe was to change his treatment of the blacks radically after writing *Really the Blues*. In "Ecstatic in Blackface," a second article on the blacks written in 1949 although not published until 1955, he again discusses the "spontaneous" black jazzman as a mythological creation of the white Negrophile which is, in its own way, as much a "lie" as that created by the southern racist. Spontaneity, as well as "Uncle Tomism," are images imposed upon the blacks to fulfill the needs of the white man, who immediately becomes critical if the black musician risks his so-called primitive spark by deviating from the "pure" music of the ghetto. Essentially, the article attacks the kind of life best exemplified by Mezz Mezzrow, whose quest for ecstasy and "authenticity" were motivated by "masochism," in the special sense of the word as used in *Limbo*. (In *The Magic of Their Singing*, moreover, it is precisely the middle-class infatuation with bohemia and the ghetto—which are falsely equated—that is satirized.) After *Really the Blues*, Wolfe rejected the romanticism of the fringe group for a more rational discussion of the psycho-sociological basis of American ambivalence toward the underdog.

Yet the black man remains, in Wolfe's fiction, a figure who attempts to breach the stereotypes created for him by society. The opening pages of *Limbo*, for instance, urge the reader to accept the racially mixed Ubu as at the very least physically "real" by describing him as the victim of tremors and insomnia. Again, in *The Late Risers*, the black protagonist, Movement, suffers not only from hypertension but from potency troubles as well, although he is continually confronted by the myth of black hyperpotency when he meets white girls.

The disappearance of the "spontaneous" black from Wolfe's work is accompanied, curiously, by a loss of the finger-snapping pace which so delightfully compensated for a lack of structure in *Really the Blues*. While later novels retain the biography's playful use of language (often to satirize jargon), Wolfe emerges as a writer of the intellect rather than of emotion. However, his novels of ideas are built around exciting and adventurous narratives and characters who are often memorable for their eccentricity and bravado. In this contrast between theme and narrative lies the problematic quality of Wolfe's work: the pull between essay and story which is never quite resolved.

II *The Plot*

Utopian science fiction had come into its own in the United States in the 1930's, during Wolfe's adolescence, and he was no doubt influenced by its popular appeal. At this time, ground was being prepared for a "serious" American work of science fiction by such British novels as Aldous Huxley's *Brave New World* (1932) and George Orwell's *1984* (1949). *Limbo* differs from either of these novels in at least two basic respects: first, its satire is directed specifically at America rather than at England; second, it has more internal "scientific" justification and, consequently, wider scope than its predecessors. Wolfe gives not only a historical and philosophical basis for the society created in his novel but also a detailed scientific and psychoanalytic background as well, including references to the influence of such figures as Norbert Wiener, Alfred Korzybski, Georg Groddeck, Edmund Bergler, and Sigmund Freud. He also uses and discusses techniques closer to the scientific ideas of the day—computerized war, lobotomy, atomic-powered prosthetics, and underground industry.

In contrast to the futuristic society described in the course of the narrative, the action of the novel begins on an uncharted island where the primitive Mandunji tribe had been brought into limited contact with technology by an American, Dr. Martine, who had arrived on the island eighteen years earlier. The Mandunji are represented by the aging Ubu, a traditionalist who looks back to the time when the islanders knew nothing of machines, and by Rambo, Martine's half-caste son, who studies medicine and is learning how to laugh—a suspect act among the sober tribesmen. In fact, any hint of the Dionysian, especially the smoking of "ganja" (marihuana), is outlawed by the Mandunji; and an offender is forced to submit to "Mandunga," a ritual involving brain surgery. Martine, who was formerly a neurosurgeon, corrects the ancient custom with the new "science" of lobotomy, which nevertheless takes the "wildness" out of its victims—along with creativity, spirit, and orgasm. Consequently, pacifism is the main characteristic of the Mandunji, who even suppress the aggression necessary for self-defense.

Midway through the novel, a flashback describes the background of Martine's sojourn on the island. He was born on July 16, 1945, near the site of the first atomic explosion in the United States and then reared as a Mormon in Salt Lake City. Eventually he went to New York City to study medicine, where he met Helder, a member of the pacifist movement. Meanwhile, the cyberneticists were rapidly developing advanced computers, until in the mid-1960's they succeeded in building EMSIAC (Electronic Military Strategy Integrator and Computer). The Russians, of course, had developed their own militarized computer in "self-defense," and so World War III, which began in 1972, was inevitable.

Under orders from the American EMSIAC, Martine left his pregnant wife, Irene, to serve on a flying hospital unit in Africa. Helder joined him, having given up pacifism during the war, as did his political colleague, Teddy Gorman, who became an ace pilot celebrated for the record number of cities he had personally bombed off the map. On October 19, 1972—the first of two dates important in the history of the new "limbo"—Martine operated on the brain of the badly wounded Teddy, whom he nicknamed "Babyface" (after the gangster Babyface Nelson) in spite of his own internal conviction that it would be better to snuff out the life of the pacifist-murderer. The same night, Martine decided that he would never again follow the instructions of an EMSIAC. Leaving his journal behind, he surreptitiously boarded a plane and flew off, by chance, to the Mandunji island. After destroying his radio and thereby relinquishing all contact with the civilization he had known, he began an eighteen-year "hibernation" with his Mandunji wife, Ooda.

The second date of consequence in *Limbo* is May 23, 1990, the day Martine decides to return to America; it is at this point that the narrative virtually begins. Strange looking white men, whom the natives call "queer-limbs," are visiting the island. Martine observes them in secret and recognizes them as Americans. Their arms and legs, however, have been replaced by artificial ones made of transparent plastic. It soon appears that the men are athletes who are able to perform impossible feats with the aid of atomic-powered (as it turns out) prosthetic limbs. After Martine discovers them taking rock samples from the island, he doubts their innocent pose as a team in training for the Olympics.

Fearing that he will be discovered on the island, Martine makes his way back to America under the guise of "Dr. Lazarus," a parasitologist, by way of a futuristic ship, the S. *Norbert Wiener.* On board, he sees the leader of the Olympic training crew, Brother Theo, and he recognizes him as the original "Babyface." Remembering that Teddy had lost his legs as well as a bit of his brain during the EMSIAC war, Martine is disturbed by the realization that Brother Theo now has no arms either. Slowly Martine learns about the world of 1990 and its "quadro-amps" through discussions with Jerry, a naïve boy serving on the ship, and through observations of New Jamestown, the largest city remaining in America. The greatest shock, however, is his discovery that a "joke" written in his wartime diary was largely responsible for the creation of the brave new world, "Limbo."

In 1972, Martine had incorporated a satire on pacifism into his journal. One of its premises was that man, being the masochistic animal he is, might voluntarily *disarm* (remove his arms) to preserve his sense of freedom during the arbitrary determinism characteristic of war. After Martine's desertion, Helder had found and read the journal and was impressed by all but what he considered to be the "joke" about masochism (which, ironically, was the only concept in the satiric portion of the journal written in sincerity). Meanwhile, Teddy had been fitted with aluminum artificial limbs, and under Helder's persuasion he bombed EMSIAC. Under the influence of Martine's journal too, Vishinu, a Russian flier and former Stalinist, bombed the Soviet EMSIAC at the same time. What was left of the world after the destruction of the militarized computers was divided into the Inland Strip (formerly midwestern America) and the East Union (part of Russia). In both locales, the pacifists quickly seized power, with Helder and Teddy at the head of the Inland Strip's government and with Vishinu at that of the East Union's.

Needing a gimmick to maintain power, the pacifists began to "martyrize" Martine in the belief that he had not deserted but had died trying to "dodge the steamroller"—a term in his journal meaning to destroy the EMSIACS, or anything which victimized man. Under the influence of Martine's "word," Teddy was the first to have his arms *voluntarily* amputated, while Helder and Vishinu followed with amputations of their legs. Soon, most of the young men in both countries were becoming "Vol-Amps" under a program called "IMMOB" ("International Mass for the Manumission of the Benign"). Following such slogans as "No Demobilization without Immobilization" and "Pacificism means Passivity" (taken out of context from Martine's journal), the whole of society became organized into a sort of caste system in which the "quadro-amp" (four-limb amputee) stood at the top, followed by "tri-amp," "duo-amp," and "uni-amp"; their prestige and their attractiveness to women depending upon how many limbs they had severed.

In the next phase of IMMOB history, the neuro-cyberneticists and the students of Norbert Wiener developed artificial limbs which were far more powerful than human ones. When their work became known, the Amps divided themselves into two parties: the Pro-Pros, who insisted that the atomic-powered prosthetics should be a reward for the Vol-Amps, and the Anti-Pros, who felt that prosthetics defeated the true purpose of IMMOB. After some violence, the Pro-Pro party became the head of government; and Helder and Teddy in America and Vishinu in Russia were fitted with the new limbs.

Meanwhile, the Amps were reading William James's *Moral Equivalent of War,* among other "pacifist" literature, with the same misguided ardor that they had read Martine's journal. Following the thought of James, they sublimated the "war instincts" partly through civil service (the most challenging being the Victoria Dredging Project, the search for the remains of Martine) and partly through the Olympic Games. The latter were less a competition between the athletic prowess of men than an engineering feat in which the latest cybernetic developments were tested. Until 1990, Brother Theo was the outstanding attraction of every game, primarily because his prosthetic limbs were technologically superior to Vishinu's. However, these "moral equivalents" really had a double purpose. Both the East Union and the Inland Strip were engaged in espionage involving columbium, a rare metal needed for the manufacture of prosthetics. Thus both the members of the Olympic training teams which toured the world and the men conscripted for civil service were metallurgists, secretly hunting for, and stealing, columbium in the name of pacifism.

In short, Martine finds that the youthful "joke" perpetuated in his diary has become the instigation for a monstrous "utopia" in which men mutilate themselves voluntarily; in which cold war between two powers threatens to become hot; and in which blacks are confined to menial jobs in the underground industries, women assume the role of sexual aggressor, laughter is rare, poetry is outmoded by slogans, intelligence is replaced by duty, and life is literally regulated by the formula "2 + 2 = 4."

For about half of the novel, Martine, like Dante's visitor to the Inferno, remains essentially a spectator. But after he has obtained some understanding of the futuristic society and admitted his share of responsibility for its creation, he shifts to an active role. The transformation takes place while he is being seduced in a most humiliating way by Neen, an artist and secret agent for Vishinu. In *Limbo,* women more or less attack the Amps, first detaching their artificial limbs and then dominating the entire sexual act. When Martine realizes that he, too, is being victimized sexually by Neen, he again says no to *that* intimate form of EMSIAC by raping her, thereby asserting his masculinity in the most admittedly "pseudo-aggressive" manner possible.

Shortly after, he falls into the hands of Vishinu, who is visiting the Inland Strip and suspects "Dr. Lazarus" of being a spy. But Martine escapes with the aid of a secret phial of Rotabunga—the Mandunji sedative—hidden in a pencil; and he flees to his birthplace, which has been converted into a shrine and rest home for the Amps. There he discovers not only that Irene and his mother are still alive but also that the son he had never seen, Tom, is the leader of the Anti-Pros. Martine leaves unrecognized after learning that Tom plans to become a castrate as another sacrifice for IMMOB.

Retiring to a deserted hunter's cabin to resolve his own psychological reactions to "Limbo," Martine watches the Olympics on television. For the first time in IMMOB history, the East Union team defeats the Inland Strippers. Shock leaves the audience unprepared for Vishinu's next move. Before accepting their trophy, the East Unioners replace their ordinary prosthetics with ones concealing weapons and proceed to attack the Inland Strip Amps. At the same time, Vishinu declares a war of liberation to free the "oppressed masses of the Inland Strip" from their "Imperialist masters." Helder immediately begins a counterattack, and bombs are soon again blotting out portions of both countries.

At this point, Martine decides he can save the situation by murdering Theo and Helder. He informs the latter of his existence through a letter with references to Rosemary—a girl Helder had raped in his youth, unknown to anyone but Martine. In the presence of Theo, Helder interviews his former roommate in Los Alamos, the capital of the Inland Strip. He begins by confessing that both the Inland Strip and the East Union had been involved in a secret arms race for years. During their talk, Theo realizes for the first time that he had been used; his devotion to IMMOB had blinded him to the true facts about the power struggle behind the slogans. Disillusioned and furious, "Babyface" lures Helder away from his guards and kills him. Meanwhile, Martine again escapes, having failed to murder Helder himself, and he sees the castrated Tom dying in the street from shrapnel wounds. As he has to, he shoots his son in the head, performing his "first successful lobotomy"—and his last. Almost immediately after, the slot beneath Los Alamos collapses in a virtual Armageddon, destroying the heart of IMMOB society.

While fleeing the city, Martine meets another Inland Stripper—Don Thurman, a member of a secret "opposition" who understands the meaning of the word "masochism" in Martine's wartime journal. Believing that Thurman and his colleagues in the East Union might now seize power and instigate a *real* peace, "Dr. Lazarus" leaves him a message revealing his identity. Martine then finds Theo, and together they steal a plane and head back to the Mandunji island. The novel ends with a speech by Rambo, who tells Ubu and the elders that there must be no more lobotomy on the island. Rather, the Mandunji must learn to understand jokes.

III *The Essay*

Wolfe's achievement in *Limbo* cannot be conveyed through a mere chronological retelling of its lengthy and complex narrative. The plot alone does not explain, for instance, why pacifism is "the subtlest kind of war," or why a society whose genesis was the destruction of an EMSIAC should immediately turn around and endorse an even more powerful and intimate machine—the prosthetic limb.

These issues are clarified in the antiutopian novel by essays interwoven with the narrative. In fact, one of the knottier critical problems about *Limbo* is the justification of its form: the book is as much an essay as it is a work of fiction. Generally, Wolfe has the ability to sustain the suspense of a story continually interrupted by philosophical discussion, but there are a few weaker moments in which essay predominates at the expense of plot. However, a delicate balance of essay and novel is typical of many works of science fiction, which often describe both realistic and extraordinary events as well as the social significance of each. But the tendency to document also can be found, often less justifiably, in Wolfe's later writing, although never to the extent of its use in his first novel.

In *Limbo,* Martine is used primarily as a talkative spectator—as a man from the world as we know it today who visits a strange land, observes it, discusses it, and assesses it before gingerly stepping across the threshold of spectator-participant. The essays are used to give the reader information about the structure and history of the future society, without which Martine's adventure is unintelligible. Technically, the discussions of IMMOB culture are carried on through such varied devices as conversations between Martine and the Amps, commentary in Martine's 1972 journal and its continuation in 1990 (called "mark i" and "mark ii," respectively), lectures at the Moral Equivalents University, demonstrations on educational television, political speeches, and letters.

Wolfe provides an appendix to the novel, "Author's Notes and Warnings," in which he acknowledges his debts to the sources of his utopian study, briefly explains his work, and then adds: "This book . . . is a rather bilious rib on 1950—on what 1950 might have been like if it had been allowed to fulfill itself, if it had gone on being 1950, only more and more so, for four more decades" (438). Characteristically, in *Limbo*'s last essay Wolfe confesses that his book was written more or less as a "rib"—a joke—and this, as we shall see, may be the keynote of the novel's meaning: the essay, as a form, is potentially a "joke" which is all too often taken seriously.

IV *The Jokes*

Limbo is, of course, more than just a satire of certain tendencies present in mid-century America and Soviet Russia. It is also, for one, a study of the "joke" per se and its role in contemporary civilization. In *Limbo,* the word "joke" appears frequently; and it is used as broadly as the context permits: at times it refers to a simple irony or to the "bellylaugh" mentioned in *Really the Blues*, a blending of tears and laughter with cathartic value. A depth-probe of the "joke," however, reveals its relationship with the absurd; life is so improbable that it is laughable. And laughter, in turn, is "the psychic snake oil which keeps the all-too-human brain from grinding itself to bits" (400).

Wolfe is most interested, however, in the way society reacts to "jokes." The very sanity of a civilization appears to depend on whether its members think jokes are funny or miss the humor and take them seriously. Moreover, in *Limbo* an inability to appreciate the absurd leads to the greatest absurdity: the virtual destruction of civilization. Martine's 1972 journal, "mark i," was written as a "joke"; but its humorless readers used it as an excuse for self-mutilation, a form of suicide symbolized by the eventual collapse of Los Alamos and by the beginning of World War IV. In part, *Limbo* contains an obvious warning to a world which has failed to laugh away the idea of an atom bomb.

Pacifism, lobotomy, EMSIAC, and IMMOB are each the products of jokes taken seriously. In the following pages we attempt to describe the three integrals of the absurd found in Wolfe's anti-utopia: the jokes, the joker, and the butts. The first of these, "The Jokes," contains a discussion of ambivalence and masochism, the media through which humor is expressed. "The Joker" involves an analysis of Martine, and "The Butts" focuses on the Amps and the Mandunji.

V *Ambivalence*

Probably the most explicit clue to the study of the absurdity found in *Limbo* is Martine's references to "ambivalence." The term is described as "Nature's joke," and thus it becomes a way of defining life: living matter, at essence, is an expression of a conflict of instincts which cannot be reconciled except in death. This quality first came to Martine's attention parabolically in the "two Mother Natures" he observed while swimming as a boy in Salt Lake. The water, which looked so soft and yielding, had defied his attempts to dive to the bottom—beneath the surface it was hard and resilient. In this ambivalent combination of masculine fistiness and feminine cushioning, Martine sensed the vigor and sparkle of life, as opposed to the "consistent" petrifaction of the alkali wastes surrounding the lake. Thereafter, in an extension of his youthful experience, he equated life with ambivalence; death, with consistency.

In his journal, Martine discusses "Ambivalent man" as the particular nemesis of the twentieth century, first described clinically in the pioneer work of Freud and by his student, Edmund Bergler. The polarities of human behavior are symbolized in *Limbo* by Rotabunga and Ganja, weeds growing on the Mandunji island, a "gift of the ambivalent gods." The former is essentially a tranquilizer, a vehicle for Apollonian restraint and vegetative calm; the latter, a cousin of marihuana—the Dionysian brew of *Really the Blues*—produces a manic state, an explosive hyperactivity. (Significantly, the Mandunji taboo ganga but endorse rota, a parody of present American law which legalizes sedatives while repressing hallucinogenics.) Rota and Ganja, the "Siamese twins" of Oceania, are externalizations of Eros and Thanatos, those warring elements which invite man to both riot and sleep at the same time.

More specifically, Martine notes that the brain is governed by two closely related drives which are loosely called "sexuality" and "aggression," [1] and that, despite all attempts to separate them, "the twain would always and everywhere meet, in every jungle, in every village, in every cell of every body—every neurone, every muscle strand, every synapse" (29). Thus, in the course of his adventure, Martine describes behavior as a hyphenation of opposites: "vertical-horizontal," "hard-soft," "activist-passivist," "I pusher-It seeker." He realizes, however, that the components are not so neatly balanced as the terms suggest; behavior is immensely complicated because the two sides of the hyphen tend to merge and overlap and to slide back into place again.

According to Martine, "Nature's joke" reached its punch line in the 1950's when man began to react against his natural ambivalence. A number of forces, including the accelerated industrial revolution and two world wars, had left the civilized world, and their microcosm on Mandunji, with what is called a "packaging mentality" in *Come on Out, Daddy* or a "monolithic view" in *The Great Prince Died.* Behind these phrases is a concept which binds *Limbo* with all of Wolfe's later work: modern man is vetoing ambivalence in favor of consistency. In trying to force a two-sided world into a one-sided pigeonhole, he is being more than just damaging; he is being suicidal, for the ultimate consistency, in theory, is the frozenness of death. But even before the fatal stage is reached, Wolfe finds a symptom of mass paranoia in a desire for consistency that attempts to accommodate everything under one program, whether it be pacifism, IMMOB, or Mandunga.

Strangely enough, this social paranoia has its roots in "another joke." The initial step in man's revolt against ambivalence is an uncompromising respect for, even worship of, "sanity." Strict traditionalism, because it too is "frozen," seems to be the only comfort against the polarities wracking the individual. Moreover, and here there is a major break with the theme of *Really the Blues*, a so-called sanity demands the suppression of the individual for the "sake" of society. But what such advocates of tradition as Ubu fail to consider (or laugh at) is that a society which defines sanity might itself be *insane*. Moreover, since each society has its own means of determining who is "sane," sanity has a purely local and arbitrary meaning.

Various aspects of sexuality, for instance, are deemed pathological by the different cultures in *Limbo*. In the first chapter, Martine refuses to lobotomize a Mandunji woman who has experienced an "unhealthy" orgasm. Irene, on the other hand, had feigned orgasm rather than be accused of the frigidity tabooed by pre-IMMOB society. Neen, following the idea of health prevalent in 1990, demands that the woman be the sexual aggressor. And Tom, whose Anti-Pro philosophy is not immediately in favor when Martine arrives in the Inland Strip, believes that movement is the antithesis of orgasm and advocates castration. Within this spectrum, only Ooda is capable both of experiencing and of enjoying orgasm, a token of true health (according to Wolfe) which surpasses cultural standards.

An overestimation of "sanity," the simplest reaction against ambivalence, is shared by the Amps and Mandunji alike. But modern man in Wolfe's antiutopia also uses his technology to far outstrip his more primitive cousins in the love of mathematical certainty. The citizens of the pre-IMMOB world, in their desperate search for the "perfectly sane," found that the machine was both perfect and sane. By its very nature, the machine is not only undivided by the tug of sexuality and aggression but is also untouched by any emotion. Because the machine "never has the jitters" (400), twentieth-century man found it the "brain's dream of fulfillment" (148) and tried to shape society in the image of an EMSIAC.

This concept is *Limbo*'s closest parallel to the themes of such other futuristic novels as Orwell's *1984* and Zamiatin's *We*. The society which emulates the machine is quickly dehumanized. A mechanistic approach to daily life leads to regulated routine, government controlled and paced with a metronome. While the Inland Strippers do not yet live in glass houses and have to chew each bite of food fifty times by law, Wolfe suggests that this kind of stifling organization might follow from the worship of the machine. Already, Helder's regime is characterized by "clock orientation" and cities with rigidly geometrical skylines. A creative intellect is repressed as thoroughly by the mechanized society as it is by the deadly traditionalism of the Mandunji.

The EMSIAC mentality came into its own, however, during World War III. The two robot brains waging the war demanded total mobilization and, consequently, nearly the entire human race was "robotized." For the first time, mankind had voluntarily forfeited all freedom of will and was activated solely by the mathematically precise orders of the cyberneticized computers. "Therein," Martine wrote in his first journal, "lies the essence of warness: the elimination of Hamletish ambivalent wavering in human affairs, the triumph of the pure hammerblow direct act. War is the engineer's answer to palsy" (203). Of course, the irony of the machine is that it too can be used ambivalently—it can harm man as much as help him. EMSIAC freed man from his dreaded decision-making—but at the cost of the destruction of most of the world. And the IMMOB state, which remains in 1990, is as much addicted to the machine-gods as ever, even though it destroyed the original EMSIACs.

In 1972, Theo and Vishinu had bombed their EMSIACs ostensibly because they feared the "steamroller" effects of the robot brains—the likelihood, according to Martine's journal, of mankind being controlled, manipulated, and victimized by a machine. The IMMOB program which followed was designed to keep the machine in its place and to eliminate the "perfect" wars the machines seem to provoke. Yet the Amps, ignoring their own ambivalence, fail to acknowledge that the "steamroller" is still secretly attractive to them. Martine recognizes this irony even in the IMMOB emblem, a figure of an Amp sitting on a steamroller, "with raised fist indomitable and the machine helplessly couchant, brought to its knees. But the man's fist was an IMMOB fist, the arm was a mesh of tubing and coils, so were all his limbs—he had subdued the machine by making himself into the machine. Peculiar sort of victory, won by incorporating the enemy into oneself. If imitation was the sincerest form of flattery, the overwhelmed machine had won the fight hands down: the master had become the mirror image of the slave" (275).

IMMOB society, then, is just another twisted version of the machine culture created previously by EMSIAC (and before that, Wolfe suggests, by ENIAC, a mathematical computer built in the 1950's by the students of Norbert Wiener). But there are special problems connected with the new IMMOB culture which insure the frustration of the Amps' dream: in yet another one of "Nature's jokes," the scanty supply of columbium (a metal basic to the manufacture of prosthetics) makes nonsense of pacifism, and the Inland Strippers and East Unioners eventually wage the "perfect" war again for what the earth refuses to yield.

In a further effort to trace the effects of society's neurotic denial of ambivalence, Martine associates the machine-culture with Mandunga in his thoughts about the history of lobotomy in the United States. When insanity became epidemic in the first half of the century, the Americans immediately turned to the machine for a cure. Shock treatment was based on the home remedy for fixing a radio—kick it! This view of the human psyche as something mechanical led to brain operations, in which "the trouble-making cogs and circuits were snipped out of the machine or at least cut off from it" (47).

Martine's training as a neurosurgeon, however, as well as his secret animal experiments on the Mandunji Island, give him the expectation, at least, that the brain, with its tens of thousands of neurological interconnections, could make EMSIAC look like a tinker toy. In this sense, those surgical shots in the dark, lobotomy and mandunga, are equally primitive and equally homicidal. The patient becomes a mental basket case whose physical counterparts in *Limbo* are Tom and the Anti-Pros, amputees without prosthetics who spend their lives in bassinets covered with blue babies' blankets. What went wrong? Faced with the problem of aggression, the IMMOB and Mandunji cultures try programmatically to remove it from human flesh, not realizing that the sexual component, aggression's twin, is cut out as well. The Amps and victims of Mandunga no longer kill, maim, or slash; but they have no sexual drive either, and consequently, no vitality. A society must, it seems, retain a sexual as well as an aggressive instinct, if only to sublimate, so that these baser forces might be replaced by their beneficent derivatives: love, creativity, health, humanism.

The twentieth-century error—the denial of humanness in favor of the machine—backfires in the end. Because a cog is just a cog in a machine, it can be removed and replaced at will. But the cogs in the human psyche have a much more complex and ambivalent function; if one or two are cut out, even to be replaced by the finest prosthetics, the human mechanism never works again. Ironically, the society which seeks a "moral equivalent of war" in ambitious civilian projects becomes a custodial society in which the unamputated women spoon-feed their helpless sons and husbands.

The ultimate "joke," then, is that ambivalence—no matter how men may react against it—is the only "consistent" fact of life. The pacifists in *Limbo* lop off arms and legs and bomb their neighbors. The destroyers of EMSIAC rivet a new machine to their bodies. The society supposedly based on humanism adopts a mechanistic view of man. Olympic Games are used as vehicles for espionage, for political maneuvering, and even for direct attack. A program for literal "disarmament" and "demobilization" ends in the development of prosthetic weapons. Even on a more personal level, ambivalence makes absurdity of man's dream of perfection. The pacifist Amps, who believe that love and goodwill are characteristic of man, have to have their artificial limbs removed before making love, lest they crush their lovers.

The most telling sign of an ambivalence that refuses to lie quietly is found in Martine's account of Amp laughter. In the window of a novelty store, mechanical Amp dolls topple when set in motion. Or Jerry, a Uni-Amp, makes a "prosthetic error" and falls. These incidents, public indications that prosthetics are less than perfect, are strangely amusing to the members of IMMOB society. Their laughter "at the symbols of their mission and the objects of their dedication" points to "ambivalence with a vengeance."

Martine speculates further and traces their amusement to the absurdity of the "communal mission" itself, which "demanded of all men within its pale that they order their psychic economies to conform with the group goal . . . : this was the meaning of the reality principle superimposed on the pleasure principle" (155).

However, the reality, in this case IMMOB, is an inadequate substitute for the pleasures of sexuality and aggression. The Amps unconsciously express their anger at the sacrifices they are forced to make by laughing at themselves. Their leaders, in turn, sense the danger of the discontent behind humor and subtly discourage it. Likewise, the Mandunji require deadpan dedication in fear of the laughter that might destroy their obsessive traditionalism.

The true nature of contemporary society as it emerges in Wolfe's antiutopia is an organized effort to compel man to sleep rather than riot. In *Come on Out, Daddy*, there is a suggestion that such an opting of Thanatos in fear of Eros is a hangover from Puritan ethics. And yet the very intensity of the program to subdue the sexual-aggressive pendulum is an indication of how close to emotional explosion modern man may be. Wolfe does not imply, however, that society's true function is to allow the individual to riot, to release the instinctual pleasures. Rather, he warns the reader that those who fight the seesaw will eventually walk the plank. Ambivalence, like it or not, is the way life expresses itself, and society must accept "Nature's joke" before such horrors as war, insanity, and the machine can be eliminated or controlled.

Neither does Wolfe's attack on contemporary technology suggest a return to primitivism. The Mandunji episodes in *Limbo* are used as a parallel to the futuristic episodes, not as an alternative to them. Although the Islanders have only the bare beginnings of an industrial revolution, Martine discovers that, like the Inland Strippers, they are victimized by their own "steamrollers." The lesson, according to Martine's journal, is not to abandon the machine, which can free man from oppressive work, but to let its use be minimal—to allow the machine to lighten man's physical burden without competing with his intellectual work; to destroy the computers and keep the tractors. Aggression, too, has its function, even in modern society, as the basis for self-defense. Rambo tells Ubu in the last chapter of *Limbo* that the young Mandunji intend to learn how to use weapons in order to keep such invaders as the Amps at their distance. Controlled aggression, it seems, is the only way the Sane can defend themselves against the more numerous Insane.

It follows that the programs rationalized by the Insane, as well as all "appeals to authority," are dangerous when the joke, warning, or inherent absurdity behind them are not recognized. Much of the "essay" of *Limbo* is devoted to an explication of the philosophies foreshadowing IMMOB, as interpreted by the Amps. For instance, while the science of prosthetics is based on the work of Norbert Wiener, the Inland Strippers ignore the scientist's warnings about the misuse of the machine, quoted in Martine's journal. Or they respond to pacifist literature without realizing that it contains the seeds of its own negation. (The writings of Gandhi, for example, treat man as an essentially benign creature, but William James finds him basically belligerent.) Or they understand as difficult a linguistic philosopher as Alfred Korzybski, who distrusted the Aristotelian absoluteness of language, but they fail to apply his theories to their particular society. Authoritative writings become, in the end, every man's *Finnegans Wake:* if man looks hard enough, he will find whatever he wants.

Of course, the most imaginative instance of a work which the Amps misuse to justify their culture is Martine's first journal, the "Basic IMMOB Text." The edition Martine reads in 1990 contains Helder's editorial comments, a drastic attempt to force the original words to fit the later interpretation.

Ironically, the one writer whom the Amps ignore is the one who could save them. Dostoevsky, whose "sickly shadow is cast over many of [*Limbo*'s] pages" (436), is resurrected in Martine. Like the Russian novelist, Wolfe's hero takes offense at the scientific "truth" of "twice two makes four" because of its disregard of all human caprice, imagination, will, or, in other words, ambivalence. The world of 1990 is Dostoevsky's nightmare fulfilled. The Amps not only insist that happiness will follow in the footsteps of science, they also cut off their limbs and even their genitalia to prove the point. And in their blind conviction, they misread the main point of Martine's journal, a reiteration of the theme of Dostoevsky's *Notes from the Underground:* the mathematical formula, consistency's altar, is "the beginning of death." The secret goal of IMMOB society, it seems, is suicide; in fact, its representatives—Helder, Tom, and Vishinu—are dead by the end of the book. Only Theo escapes, because, like Rambo, he is the heir to Martine's mission: he must return to "save" the world of 1991.

VI *Masochism*

The theme of ambivalence has a long and respectable literary history reaching from Shakespeare to Saul Bellow. However, those works dealing with man in conflict with himself have usually treated human behavior in terms of good-evil, mind-body, love-duty, and, in much of contemporary literature, activity-passivity. Wolfe, by contrast, is probably among the first novelists to call a spade a spade: his contribution to the theme involves a psychoanalytic study in which his protagonists are frankly called "Ambivalent" men. The specific horror of *Limbo* is again a psychoanalytic one—the fictionalization of that kind of masochism certain psychoanalysts have diagnosed as a contemporary epidemic. This is not the sexual perversion associated with the Marquis de Sade and with Sacher Masoch, but a more embracing form variously called "moral" (Freud), "social" (Theodor Reik), or "psychic" masochism (Edmund Bergler). The neurosis might be defined as an enjoyment of pain that is both unconscious and suprasexual. Unlike the pervert, who may be whipped to orgasm, the psychic masochist *seems* to be a victim of fate whose life is continually made unbearable by "accidental" misfortune or hardship "imposed" by enemies. Actually, the "injustices" are unconsciously courted by the neurotic so that he may gain pleasure at the price of conscious pain.

In *Limbo,* the psychic "joke," in which the "pratfaller" deliberately trips over his own foot, is a companion to "Nature's joke," ambivalence. However, while ambivalence is common to life in all states, the "self-maiming" tendency is peculiar to man alone. Moreover, the latter is a disease, a mental malfunctioning in which reality is significantly distorted. Wolfe's antiutopia envisions society as a product of these two forces, one natural, the other unnatural. And masochism, it turns out, is the secret nourishment on which such other man-made "evils" as war, advanced technology, and lobotomy feed.

Why masochism? Wolfe had been *profoundly* influenced by the writings of his analyst, Edmund Bergler, who developed the theory of "psychic masochism" after reading Freud's controversial *Beyond the Pleasure Principle.* Although Bergler admits to having treated more than thirty professional writers in his book on the subject, *Psychoanalysis of Writers* (New York, 1954), Wolfe is the only known writer to acknowledge the analyst as a source for material used in his work.[2] Not only is Bergler referred to by name and quoted in the text of *Limbo,* but a table entitled "Aggression: True and False," which originally appeared in at least three of the analyst's books, is reproduced in full. The antiutopia's indebtedness to Bergler frequently borders on psychoanalytic propaganda. In his "Author's Notes and Warnings," Wolfe writes, "For purposes of this book I have assumed that, by the mid-sixties, analytic thought had pretty much come around to the ideas and emphases worked out by Dr. Bergler" (437). Unfortunately, perhaps, the analyst, who died in 1962, does not seem to have attracted a following beyond the 1950's.

In Bergler's view, "psychic masochism" is the "basic neurosis" from which such varied troubles as homosexuality, impotence, frigidity, divorce, writer's block, criminosis, suicide, and prostitution stem. While Wolfe deals with all of these "neurotic rescue stations," if not in *Limbo* then in later novels, with great explicitness, his description of "psychic masochism" itself is complete but fragmented throughout Martine's journals. Because the theory is crucial for an understanding of *Limbo,* and especially for an analysis of Martine's character, it is reconstructed in the following paragraphs.[3]

In the last phase of his career, Freud offered the thesis of instinctual duality to explain such previously irreconcilable refutations of the pleasure principle as "repetition compulsion" (the compulsion to repeat *un*pleasant experiences from the past). Many of his students, including Jung, could find no evidence for a "death instinct" which was supposedly antipathetic to both life and the pleasure principle (the "sexual" or self-preservative instinct). Bergler, however, not only accepted the duality of Thanatos-Eros, the "Siamese twins" of the psyche, but added his own refinements to Freud's theory. According to Bergler, it is the function of Eros to turn Thanatos from the individual to the outer world. But Eros is only partially successful, and there remains a residue of Thanatos which is inimical to the ego. In the most simplistic sense, the instinctual portion turned outward is "aggressive"; that turned inward is "masochistic"; although neither exists in "pure form."

On this theoretic foundation, Bergler built his concept of "psychic masochism"—a view of man as an "injustice collecting" animal. The description of the "self-maiming" tendency is divided into two parts: the "generic picture," its development through infancy; and the "clinical picture," its symptomatic expression in the neurotic. The former is carefully documented in *Limbo* within Martine's analyses of his own childhood. The newly born infant, whose only desire is for total inertia (a form of death), is the victim of a fallacy called "infantile megalomania:" the belief that he is entirely self-sufficient and in control of the "universe." As such, the "intrusion" of milk and of even his involuntary bodily functions are construed as "blows" to his megalomania. The infant reacts by trying to show aggression (as Thanatos is turned outward) which is completely ineffective. As the infant becomes a child, however, even this aggression is inhibited by parental punishment and subsequent guilt. The healthy child then compromises by subliminating aggression and by finding a mitigated pleasure in nondestructive ways.

The neurotic child, on the other hand, remains aggressive and refuses to relinquish his grandiose megalomania. But the punishment he receives has to be reconciled with the pleasure principle. He solves this dilemma by unconsciously turning pain into pleasure so that suffering becomes enjoyable. At the same time, the neurotic is haunted by the infantile nightmare—the "septet of baby fears"—in which the pre-Oedipal mother is seen as a murderer, whose very milk is first a "poison," then a pleasure to be refused.[4] For the "psychic masochist," who believes his mother to have been the Great Refuser, the world becomes a dramatization of refusal and punishment.

This original feeling of being deprived and hurt by the mother (even if she were good in reality) is compulsively repeated in the "clinical picture" of "psychic masochism." But in the adult, the superego ("unconscious conscience") objects to the enjoyment of suffering, and the masochistic ego is forced to defend itself in order to achieve its aim. It does so through "pseudo-aggression," a threefold subterfuge designed to "bribe" the superego with conscious suffering that may be *unconsciously* enjoyed. The masochist first of all provokes a situation in which he will be refused. Second, he displays "pseudo-aggression," a mock-anger at the refuser. Third, he indulges in self-pity and unconscious pleasure at having been refused, just as the neurotic child once took pleasure in having been punished by his mother. This elaborate defense is successful only because the neurotic's superego is "corrupt." The healthy superego, by contrast, will not accept the bribe of "pseudo-aggression" and self-pity, and any masochistic residue is forcibly repressed.

According to Wolfe, "psychic masochism" is a "joke" because the "pseudo-aggression" involved is a "lie," a mere parody of the natural aggression which is used only in self-defense and never for masochistic purposes. The offensive wars, the rape episodes, voluntary amputation, brain operations, the "humanist" battle against the machine, indeed "ninety-nine percent" of aggression, all are the lies that the corrupt superego of civilization demands of its truly passive individuals. Likewise, the myth of the refusing mother becomes the IMMOB "lie" writ large: the rarity of columbium is interpreted by the Amps as a refusal of "Mother" nature, and a "pseudo-aggressive" war is waged to conceal their secret delight. In the reality of *Limbo,* most mothers, nature and otherwise, are generous; but their sons, dissuaded by their self-induced masochistic "hoax," will not see them that way.

Their unwillingness to look beyond the "septet of baby fears" is consciously realized by a denial of ambivalence and a yearning for consistency. "Megalomania" is, in fact, synonomous with consistency for Wolfe. The infant who believed he was the center of an all-inclusive *uni*verse, which did not allow for the existence of even his mother, becomes, in the adult "megalomaniac," the compulsive repeater of the erroneous idea that society is a mathematically reducible unit. Thus, while the sociological reaction against ambivalence takes the form of an overestimation of "sanity" and the norm, the *psychological* reaction contradicts it with the masochistic breakdown. In short, Wolfe implies, man would rather cut off his limbs for masochistic pleasure than destroy his fantasy of megalomania and his desire for consistency.

The distinction created in this study between ambivalence and masochism is a false one, for the neurosis is indeed composed of the polarities Eros-Thanatos, pleasure-pain, generic-clinic. The very fact that "compulsive repetition" is a part of human experience suggests that man wants to retreat to the past as well as to move ahead to the future. But such distinctions are expedient even for Wolfe, who analyzes the elements of 1990 society from both points of view. In the second half of *Limbo,* a psychoanalytic interpretation of society is added to the sociological. This function is the primary one of Martine's journal, which, although written in 1972, remains the last word about the futuristic culture that annotates it.

According to the thought expressed in Martine's first journal, "mark i," man has *always* been a masochistic animal, although the names of his "persecutors" have changed from "demons, furies, witches, ghosts, God, the elements, fate, Karma, kismet, germs, ruling classes, id, norns" (205) to "steamroller" in IMMOB society. The entire rostrum of supposed fate-dispensers is summed up for the Amps by the "It," [5] a force hostile to the "I." But before EMSIAC, the mythic "It" was never well enough established as clearly distinct from the "I" so that man could achieve his secret aim of total inertia. However, except for an occasional Mandunga, man had enough masochistic satisfaction from the punitive forces of nature, disease, and hard labor to keep from destroying himself altogether.

With the advent of modern technology, this situation changed. When nature was conquered and even made to work for the *good* of mankind, EMSIAC, along with robot culture and H-bombs, "had to be invented in order that man could go on feeling sorry for himself" (206). The destruction of EMSIAC, in this sense, was a "pseudo-aggressive" gesture, to be replaced by the more culturally acceptable prosthetic limb. But the machine, whether controlled by EMSIAC or attached to the human body, becomes the first *real* victimizer in the history of mankind; and the Amps are at last able to become the basket cases that man has always yearned to be.

War, too, is seen by Martine as a compulsive repetition of the nursery situation. In the computerized war in particular, the infant's sense of victimization is realized. The wounds received and the death that threatens are the "septet of baby fears" all over again as well as a "blow" to the sense of dignity (or "megalomania"). Secretly, the adult neurotic achieves masochistic pleasure from this dangerous form of passivity. But, unlike the infant, his aggressive reaction, "pseudo" or otherwise, *is* effective: "In a sense, war is an institution which allows men-regressed-to-infants to murder their mommies, the job they muffed in the nursery" (212). In reality, of course, they murder only each other, for any backtracking in psychic time involves self-destruction. With this all-too-serious thought in mind, Martine suggested his satiric "solution": men should receive their wounds *voluntarily* to avoid the initial victimization. But taken literally, voluntary amputation is just masochism officially approved. If, in the final analysis, wars are strictly man-made, *all* wounds can be thought of as voluntary.

The aggression, then, that is concealed behind pacifism, mandunga, and everything that *Limbo* satirizes, is ideally directed against a dangerous archetypal and mythic White Goddess. In the society of 1990, Martine discovers, "women are the new IMMOB steamrollers" (246), because men secretly want them to be. In this sense, voluntary amputation represents the ultimate sexual ploy of the "psychic masochist," who unconsciously provokes a threatening aggression in his women by himself remaining passive. In fact, during sexual foreplay, the women characteristically remove the Amp's prosthetic limbs, a symbolic quadro-castration that ends in a reversal of roles which is humiliating and masochistically pleasurable for the man (as well as unsatisfactory for the woman). Moreover, in that final flowering of IMMOB that is represented by the Anti-Pros, voluntary castrates and basket cases, the Oedipal mother and her projection in the sexually desirable woman are replaced by the custodial, pre-Oedipal mother, a "murderer" whose essence is "denial." For Tom and his fellow addicts of the crib, women cease to be sexually attractive; orgasm is, instead, associated with what is called the "oceanic": a sense of oneness with the universe derived from a so-called mature megalomania (and at the price of one's limbs and manhood).

But are not the mothers, who were so closely involved with those crucial, formative years of the Toms, Theos, and Helders somehow to blame for IMMOB society after all? Again, Wolfe's view is influenced by Bergler and by the British school of analysts: "There are sins of the sons too!" (282). According to Bergler, infant education has little to do with the formation of character, for a *good* environment does not necessarily produce a non-neurotic person. The deciding factor is, rather, a combination of the intensity of a child's instincts, his fantasies and distortions of reality, and the effectiveness of his "septet of baby fears." In placing the responsibility for neurosis in the hands of the sons, Wolfe anticipates the confrontation of the Marxist theory of environmental determination and the Existential view of individual responsibility, which becomes a central theme of *In Deep*.

Responsibility's opposite, for Wolfe, is always represented by a yearning for death, the implicit meaning of the adult "megalomania": "Call his mirage the ecstasy of sainthood, Brahman, Yoga, Vedanta, Tao, IMMOB, what you will: it's still the same old wearisome death instinct. And so is the communist yearning for the oblivion of the proletarian herd or the American yearning for the oblivion of the Jonesian herd, and for the same reasons. All ways of evading the alienating sheath of skin by signing the 'I's' death warrant. People afraid of standing on their own two feet, of living with the impossible anguished tension of humanness" (413–14).

The clash of "Ambivalent Man" and "Masochistic Man" in *Limbo* leaves both the primitive and the civilized world in a shambles. The programmatic elimination of the "insane," the control of human behavior by mathematical formula, the desire for consistency that ignores human polarity, the mechanistic attitude—all are attempts to evade responsible maturity and to return instead to the undissolved megalomania of the newly born infant (or better yet, to the all-comforting womb) where no number larger than one exists. And, in the course of the narrative, lobotomies are performed, EMSIACS are developed, world wars are waged, atomic weapons destroy cities, Olympic Games turn into battlefields, espionage threatens peace—all to "prove" to the corrupt social superego that death is not yearned for at all. Meanwhile, men become voluntary basket cases and surreptitiously enjoy the crib with society's pat on the back as the final "joke."

Yet, despite Wolfe's treatment of man as essentially self-defeating, *Limbo* ends optimistically. The forces of "evil" are destroyed: Helder, Tom, and Vishinu are dead as well as many of the Amps; Theo has been "converted"; Neen has recognized, if not achieved, the healthiest form of sexuality; Ubu and the elders have been politely ousted by Rambo and the younger Mandunji. Meanwhile, the forces of "good" have survived: Don Thurman waits for his chance to correct the remains of IMMOB society; Ooda is pregnant; Martine returns to the Mandunji island with a "new son"—Theo. Moreover, there is the example of Martine himself, a "psychic masochist" who "finds himself" and, in the course of the action, achieves a self-cure. Wolfe even provides a number of strategies for fighting psychic masochism. First, accept Martine's credo—"Don't be a victim—of the outside *or* of yourself—

and don't victimize anyone else" (55). Second, recognize ambivalence, but follow Rimbaud's advice to the Lesbians—"Shun the Infinity in you!" (190), especially the death instinct. Third, avoid the "ninety-nine percent" of violence that is "pseudo-aggression," as outlined in the table Rambo shows to the elders. Finally, learn how to laugh, particularly at machines and at textbooks—"steamrollers" cannot survive unless taken seriously.

Wolfe's explicit optimism in the midst of the social crisis he satirizes may be, at least partially, another borrowing from Bergler, who, in *The Battle of Conscience* (1948), finds no scientific reason for accepting a pessimistic outlook—because there has been no clinical proof to date that humanity will destroy itself. There is also an echo of Dostoevsky in the brightness of the last pages of *Limbo:* if life is absurd, it follows that "anything is possible." Even in a society as oppressive as the Inland Strip, a secret opposition does exist and can even hope to win in the end. Even a murderer like Theo can be transformed into a "healthy" individual. Even if Thanatos appears to have the upper hand, Eros can stage an insurrection. Implicit in the theme of ambivalence is that the authoritarian system will contain its rebel, and this applies both to society and to the individual psyche. Thus, for all their similarities of plot, Wolfe's *Limbo* stands apart from the pessimism of Orwell's *1984* and Zamiatin's *We,* in which political opposition is manufactured by the government and no free will is possible. While the latter were intended merely to satirize certain political and psychological attitudes, *Limbo* has a clear didactic purpose that is based on the idea that human nature *can* change.

Wolfe's dynamic view of the psyche indicates that mankind can be made healthier, not—as the Amps supposed—happier. As Dostoevsky and, later, Zamiatin realized, happiness is not only impossible, it is not even entirely desirable. Wolfe's view rests heavily on Freud's *Civilization and Its Discontents,* which postulates that society and instinctual satisfaction are inimical. In fact, many of IMMOB's futile attempts to find happiness are taken from the list in Freud's book: isolation from human relations; Yogi (practiced by the Anti-Pros), which tries to annihilate the instincts; scientific protection against the suffering that nature imposes; the transference of instinctual aims to less frustrating intellectual work; the creation of a "utopia" to correct the world's evils;

the "religion" which urges everyone to accept its single road to happiness while distorting reality; and, when all else fails, psychosis.

In this context, Freud also mentions the "happiness" erroneously attributed to primitive people by those disillusioned with society. In *Limbo,* Wolfe treats the primitive Mandunji as a neurotic culture, whose frustrations are very similar to that imposed upon civilized societies, thus breaking the stereotype popularized by Jean-Jacques Rousseau, Herman Melville, and Paul Gaugin. Furthermore, Wolfe even attributes his thoughts about the machine culture in his "Author's Notes and Warnings" to a literal reading of Freud's remarks in the above-mentioned book: "Man has become a god by means of artificial limbs, so to speak, quite magnificent when equipped with all his accessory organs; but they do not grow on him and they still give him trouble at times. However, he is entitled to console himself with the thought that this evolution will not come to an end in A.D. 1930. Future ages will produce further great advances in this realm of culture . . . " (437). Wolfe deliberately takes Freud's "joke" seriously (for literary purposes), thus demonstrating, as his satire enters its final improbable convolution, that even "jokes" can be creatively misused.

VII *The Joker*

If the Amps, like futuristic Madame Bovaries, have been corrupted by literature (or have used literature as an excuse for corruption), is the literature to blame for their fate? Martine calls his first notebook—the IMMOB "bible"—a "dirty joke" which is to some extent responsible for the "obscenity" of life in 1990. In his second notebook, written nearly twenty years after the first one, Martine finally recognizes the motivation behind his own writing: "IMMOB is the full flowering of man's capacity for masochism. Born of a joke that miscarried. All right—but then, doesn't that mean the joke itself was a pretty revealing one? The kind of joke nobody but an eighteen-karat masochist—trying to shrug off his own flaw by making a joke of it, in the spirit of *l'humeur noir*—would have thought of? " (319). Martine's notebook, it turns out, was written by "Masochistic Man in person" (319), hence its "charisma" : it dramatized the neurosis with which everyone secretly identifies.

With the emphasis on "psychic masochism," everything about

Martine's life has correspondences with Bergler's generic and clinical pictures. Like IMMOB, Martine was "born of a joke that miscarried": in late pregnancy, his mother had joined his father, a professor of radiological medicine, at Alamogordo—the site of the first experimental detonation of an atomic bomb. When the explosion occurred on July 16, 1945, Martine was born two months prematurely. The implication is that the premature infant, "cheated" by his mother out of the womb time due him, would have sensed an "injustice" from the beginning—if not from the birth trauma itself, then from the *myth* of the birth trauma learned in childhood when, Martine recalls, his mother "reconstructed it for me many times" (62).

Furthermore, such an infant, because he would be even weaker than "normal" infants, would find his early aggression all the more ineffectual, and would be inclined to seek an alternative by turning aggression inward, replacing fury with masochism. Wolfe uses the details of Martine's birth to reflect the larger genesis of the nuclear age: the atomic bomb was also born too soon, in the sense that society was not yet able to limit its nondestructive potential. Likewise, when the protest against the bomb—which may "cheat" civilization of its future—had no effect, anger was internalized and men destroyed themselves instead of the weapons they could not reach.

With the tendency toward masochism established, Martine's case history continues with some remarks about his parents. Both were kind to the boy, although they were inveterate "injustice collectors" themselves. Martine Senior is described as a "Good American father" whose delight was the weekend fishing trip: the flight from women to the self-sufficient world of "masculine brotherhood," a nostalgic re-creation of earliest infancy and its belief that the threatening mother does not exist. Mrs. Martine is one of the most shadowy figures in *Limbo,* no doubt in contrast to her greater mythic significance, but Wolfe does suggest that she took her husband's weakness as her own "virus"—as an "injustice" personally directed at her. Of greater importance to the futuristic society, however, is the Mormon education they gave their son. Martine calls his original desire to keep a notebook a "messianic urge." "I'm a sucker for saving civilizations—it's the Mormon in me" (254). It is not until the last pages of *Limbo* that he recognizes the element of megalomania in messiahdom, which becomes "a technique for self-extinction under the banner of saving others from extinction" (387).

In short, Martine is less motivated by the rather pale characters of his parents than by his own fury, which he projects onto his environment. Reality becomes falsely threatening; and, as he grows older, Martine secretly enjoys his "enforced" passivity. Meanwhile, his mother remains the menacing figure of the "septet of baby fears"—a "murderer" who "refuses" food, shelter, clothing, love, who never "gives" at all. "What he really had against his mother was not this or that real hurt but—her very existence. Her mere existence as Other, her 'refusal' to be co-opted and absorbed by him" (290). Eventually, this basic myth is stabilized for Martine in a specific childhood incident, re-created during his visits to his birthplace and the hunter's cabin in 1990. Martine's spontaneous memory of the long-repressed event is one of the climaxes toward which the narrative of *Limbo* reaches.

In early childhood, young Martine becomes ill and is delirious for three days. When the crisis passes and he regains consciousness, his first impression is that "some malevolent thing . . . had been deliberately done to him" (288). Immediately, he sees his mother sitting by his bedside; and in a "weak, martyrish voice," he asks for his favorite chocolate cake. When his mother explains that broth would be better, young Martine becomes so furious that the doctor is forced to inject him with an opiate while his mother holds him down. In 1990, the adult Martine is able to understand the unconscious significance of the incident. The word "virus" had meant nothing to the child; it seemed to him that a hostile, external agent had robbed him of self-sufficiency, forcing him to depend again on his mother for his most basic functions. His helplessness was a dramatic revival of earliest infancy, when dependency had been construed as a "blow" to megalomania.

Furthermore, like the infant, he was too weak to express effectual anger at his loss of dignity. At the same time, his mother became the pre-Oedipal "murderer," who, he imagined, had deliberately caused his misfortune. This impression of abuse, however, was unconsciously enjoyed after certain concessions were made to appease his superego (the "clinical picture"): first, young Martine provoked a situation in which he would be refused by asking for chocolate cake. Second, he "defended himself" against the refuser (his mother) with "pseudo-aggression" (his tantrum).

Third, he was able to indulge in masochistically enjoyed self-pity and pain (the injection) while reaffirming the myth "that it was his mother who was descending upon him with a murderous needle in hand, needle, knife, dagger, something" (289).

Martine's "basic fallacy" (Bergler's term) of Mother the Murderer is used in *Limbo* as a specific reflection of the archetypal fallacy underlying contemporary culture in which Mother Nature is construed as hostile to her natural children, whom she deliberately made imperfect (ambivalent). And if men pretend to flee from the "murderer" to the "safer," more "perfect" quarters of the machine, the self-destruction involved is the giveaway: deeper than the fear of the pre-Oedipal mother is the need to continually resurrect her in order to prove her treachery repeatedly. Thus, the antiutopia's technology is secretly created in the image of the "murderer" so that the "basic fallacy" might be perpetuated: "It had to be faced: the myth of having been denied would not be nourished so devotedly, and enacted in adult life over and over so compulsively, if under it was not the deeper desire to be refused, to precipitate refusals: under the protest is the yearning—a strategy for courting pain" (291). Borrowing again from Bergler, Martine concludes that if the hostile mother had really existed, instead of having been masochistically invented, one would attempt to *avoid* pain in maturity. But the neurotic becomes an "addict of pain" (291) whose *pleasure* is to re-enact the myths of the denied chocolate cakes.

Henceforth, the events of Martine's life are seen as a voluntary repetition of his early illness and of his mother's "refusal"—a sometimes active, sometimes passive reconstruction of the mythic incident. For instance, his choice of a career in neurosurgery allowed him to use hypodermic needles on others, a "pseudo-aggressive" pretense of revenge for his youthful passivity at the hands of his doctor and mother. His marriage to Irene, a frigid woman who refused him sexually, was also an invocation of his "refusing" mother. Even his relationship with Helder before 1972 was masochistically motivated: Martine's conscious antipathy to pacifist philosophy was nullified by his choice of the leader of the Pacifist party for a roommate. Beyond its political significance, the term "pacifism" reminded Martine of his helplessness in infancy and of his ambivalent desire to both escape and return to an inert state. His intellectual attacks on the pacifist movements were, again, a "pseudo-aggressive" reaction against the emotional passivity he was constantly provoking in order to assure "refusal."

The relationship between Martine and Helder had come to a head after the suicide of Rosemary. One evening in the 1960's, Helder had brutally raped his girlfriend after making a speech at a pacifist rally. Upon his return to his room, where he confessed to Martine, the police had arrived with news of Rosemary's suicide. Helder denied being with the girl after the rally, and Martine had hesitatingly confirmed his story. Later, in 1990, Martine therapeutically recalls Helder's motives as well as his own. If rape is interpreted as a "pseudo-aggressive" attempt to escape passivity at the hands of a woman, the character of the "rapist-in-the-pacifist" can be studied on three levels: "(a) the passive-feminine masochistic baby, intent on repeating with all persons and objects in its environment its nursery myth of the denying mother; (b) as a defense against that, the extremely active-aggressive tough guy; (c) as a secondary defense against *that,* the humanitarian pacifist . . . " (341).[6] Nevertheless, Martine had collaborated the alibi Helder had given the police, an indication that the role of rapist was as secretly comforting to Martine as the role of pacifist. The truth of this concealed identification is exposed more than twenty years later when Martine more or less rapes Neen.

Until 1972, Martine had continued to arrange his life as a recreation of his basic fallacy. But, during the EMSIAC war, his secret desire to be victimized was spectacularly realized. Perhaps the trauma created by the machine-war was able to satisfy his masochistic needs; at any rate, he was able to achieve a temporary cure on October 18 of that year when he said "No" to EMSIAC, a foreshadowing of the grand "No" of the society which destroyed EMSIAC shortly after. This very significant attempt to refuse victimization was followed, however, by eighteen years of "hibernation"—total passivity—on the Mandunji Island. During this interval, his neurosis became progressively destructive: he practiced lobotomy on the innocent islanders, obviously more for his needs than for theirs. At the same time, he reacted against the warmth of his Mandunji wife, Ooda, preferring the mythic Refuser to the real Giver. Specifically, he used their sexual relationship for neurotic purposes rather than for pleasure. While Ooda gave herself to the sexual act in a total way, Martine removed himself from ultimate pleasure by adopting an esthetic attitude toward sexuality rather than by losing himself in the physical experience. By making an abstraction of Ooda's love—a love he could recognize only intellectually—he could divorce himself from it and, consequently, retain his real desire for rejection. His behavior, furthermore, was unconsciously meant to be provocative, and, of course, Ooda occasionally responded with the refusal Martine masochistically enjoyed.

This situation is changed when Martine decides to return to America, supposedly in fear of discovery by the Amps and of subsequent punishment for his desertion in 1972. On a less rational level, however, his journey is meant to precipitate a kind of self-therapy and cure; appropriately, therefore, his adventures in the Inland Strip are punctuated by meaningful dreams, depression, physical deterioration, and spontaneous recollections of previously repressed childhood events—all the common symptoms of effective therapy as described by Bergler in *The Basic Neurosis* (1949). If Martine's neurosis seems to worsen after leaving the Mandunji Island, where passivity was reinforced by the association of primitivism and infancy, it is because the sick and healthy portions of his ego are carrying on a psychic war to decide the future of his "basic fallacy." The eventual predominance of health is achieved at the expense of the myth of Mother the Murderer, a myth which is destroyed in several stages toward the end of *Limbo.*

In the first phase, Martine has been pretending to be drugged when he sees Neen approaching him with a pin. With unwarranted fury, he attacks her, "wondering all the while he was hurting her why the image of the pin in her plunging hand still clung to his eyeballs, why it made him want to kill this woman" (265), and he finishes by calling her "Rosemary." Here the childhood trauma and pseudo-aggressive revenge of the rapist come fleetingly to life before being submerged again in the obscurity of the unconscious.

In the second phase, Martine has been discovered outside of his birthplace; and, although his mother and Irene do not recognize him, they place their delirious guest in Martine's childhood bed. In his quasi-conscious state, Martine sees the two women and the doctor descending upon him to inject a sedative, and despite his panic, he almost succeeds in equating the incident with his childhood trauma.

The third phase takes place in the deserted hunter's cabin, where Martine "hunts" for the connection between his recent hallucinations in his birthplace and the past. It is then that he spontaneously remembers his youthful illness, the basis for the mythic belief that his *mother* had tried to kill him with a hypodermic needle. At the same time, he is able to relate the myth to various events in his life and to *refute* it through his understanding.

Immediately after, he has a dream in which "everything happening was in the nature of a pun" (292), or, rather, like a pun the dream *condensed* everything he had been unconsciously associating with his mother and needles. But after the horrors mount in the dream, "Rambo leaned over and administered the antidote" (293); and he thanked his son, saying, "A myth is as good as a smile" (293). Before slipping into a deep, therapeutic sleep, Martine dreams of Rambo and Ooda, who urge him to "forget about needles and the need for needles and the need to cover up for needles" (293).

Dr. Martine's second notebook ("mark ii"), written in the hunting lodge after his sleep, may be regarded, in a Berglerian sense, as the writing of a non-neurotic person. The "dirty joke" of "mark i," a product of masochism, is conspicuously absent in the 1990 journal, which is primarily concerned with the history of IMMOB as well as a knowledgeable discussion of ambivalence and masochism. The giant "NO" Martine said to EMSIAC in 1972 is now replaced by a far more affirmative "YES," this time to the "Hyphen"—the acceptance of ambivalence, which is the only way to fight the EMSIACs of man's own making. But, before the "dirty joke" can be transformed into healthy laughter, Martine performs a few largely symbolical acts meant to exorcise the remnants of his neurosis.

First, he kills his son Tom, the "sin of his sin," who is mortally wounded anyway. Because Tom looks just like his father, Martine thinks of him as a physical realization of his own psychic disease. As such, the killing is metaphorically necessary for the healthy Martine who thus takes leave of his neurotic self. On a less symbolic level, Tom's death marks Martine's first destructive act that is not "pseudo-aggressive" (in terms of the table reprinted in *Limbo*). It is a disagreeable necessity which has no connection with masochistic pleasure. Nevertheless, Martine asks if he would have "pulled the trigger if Tom Martine . . . had not been mortally wounded? Unspeakable question, answer in the echo cave" (376). The former lobotomist is very much aware of his capacity for murder if the masochistic elements of his ego were ever to erupt again.

If Martine loses a son during his cure (one he never knew at that), the gains of health compensate for his former "pleasure." There is, of course, Rambo waiting for him on the Mandunji Island, where Ooda, we learn in the last pages of *Limbo,* is expecting the birth of a new child. Moreover, Martine more or less adopts Theo, whom he helps to cure of psychic masochism as well. Don Thurman, the leader of the opposition in the Inland Strip, is associated with Martine's father, found again in the midst of IMMOB ruin. Finally, there is Ooda, herself, whose love is felt to be one of the rewards of health. Bergler, in a chapter from *The Battle of Conscience,* "Tender Love—The Classical Antidote for Guilt," explains that love absorbs the impetus for masochism by seeming to restore megalomania and its delusions of grandeur. Following this thought, the importance of what might be called "the small beginning" becomes evident in Wolfe's fiction. Like Martine, most of Wolfe's heroes leave their respective "limbos" to live in an underdeveloped country or island where they may devote themselves to the pleasures of monogamy. There the combination of love and hard work strengthens the ego, thus preventing a return of neurosis.

"The small beginning" suggests that there is more to gain in achieving a workable relationship with one other person of the opposite sex than in participating in large-scale "humanitarian" programs. Significantly, Martine refutes the underlying destructive nature of the "messianac urge" by destroying his second notebook after leaving the Inland Strip. Similarly, heroes of later novels renounce political aspirations or commercial success, replacing them with the self-satisfaction of creativity uncorrupted by advanced technology, by financial incentives, or by a hunger for power. At the same time, they can enjoy a natural laughter (the "bellylaugh") which is *not* motivated by masochistic jokes; instead, such a laugh is associated with the release of tension often equated with true orgasm[7] in Wolfe's work. In essence, it signifies the victory of Eros—the sexual and life instincts—and the failure of Thanatos to control the individual.

The very optimism at the end of *Limbo* participates in this victory. In retrospect, Wolfe's novel appears to be thematically more concerned with therapy than with the disease satirized. The emphasis, as it turns out, is on civilization curing itself by allowing its neurotic elements to cancel each other out. Moreover, the "happy ending" is not based on the sort of expedient coincidence seen in H. G. Wells's *The War of The Worlds,* in which the Martians suddenly die because of a lack of immunity to supposedly innocuous earth germs just as they are about to destroy the earth's inhabitants. Wolfe avoids the easy answer by making a *real* utopia, whose establishment is hinted at in the last pages of *Limbo,* contingent upon the destruction of most of the world. The choice, for Wolfe, seems to be between the optimism of such neo-Freudians as Bergler, for whom pessimism itself is neurotic, and the darker vision of Freud, who, in *Civilization and Its Discontents,* considered therapy for society as a whole impossible. *Limbo* finally refutes the last point of view by standing under the wing of Dostoevsky, whose belief in the absurd makes anything possible—even a utopia.

VIII *The "Butts"*

Limbo is basically a novel concerning the adventures of one character—Martine. The other protagonists exist, not as people, but first of all as vehicles for ideas, and second, as the various components which comprise Martine's very ambivalent and complex personality. But however fleetingly the lesser characters are treated, they are often unique in that they break the stereotypes created by such popular literary forms as science fiction. Characteristically for Wolfe, *Limbo* thus satirizes bad books as well as the society that creates them. Ooda, for instance, is not the grass-skirted lotus eater, the grinning slave of her man—as such island girls are often portrayed; she is a thirty-six-year-old woman, capable of depression, anger, and cynicism as well as of love. Furthermore, she is a radical within her own environment who smokes the forbidden "ganja" and is otherwise "different" from her contemporaries—an indication that even among primitives it is possible, at least, to tell one woman from another. Likewise, Jerry and Theo are not merely the sloganizing devotees of the party line usually found in antiutopian literature, as in the lesser characters of Zamiatin's *We;* instead, they are moved by a sort of boy-scout enthusiasm. Wolfe tries to throw his readers off balance by treating character types generally thought of as "innocent" as the manipulators of atomic bombs. In later novels, however, the ironic use of or departure from the stereotype becomes a frontal attack on mass media and "hack" writing in which characterization is predictably "consistent."

Part of Wolfe's craftsmanship in *Limbo* is his economic use of characters who are not permitted to be literary clichés. Although the novel is concerned with two cultures, and within the "civilized" society alone there are two powers, two parties, and an Opposition, the book is miraculously unburdened by a large number of characters. Martine speaks at length to only six others in the Inland Strip (Jerry, Neen, Theo, Helder, Don Thurman, and an unidentified Anti-Pro), while three others appear briefly (Tom, Vishinu, Irene). Similarily, the Mandunji are realized by a mere three characters: Ubu, Rambo, and Ooda. But even among these few, Tom, Don Thurman, Rambo, and Helder achieve prominence only in the last chapters of *Limbo*; and fully two-thirds of the novel is limited to Martine and six significant characters. Yet, the quantitative economy of Wolfe's protagonists belies the complexity of the attitudes they represent. Neen, for example, is used to typify: (1) a citizen of the East Union, (2) an espionage agent, (3) an artist employed by the state, (4) a woman in IMMOB society, (5) a neurotic whose main symptom is "frigidity"; furthermore, she provides information about the suppression of blacks in the Inland Strip, Amp entertainment, and the "new" sexuality in which women take the masculine role.

Despite their functional multiplicity, many of the lesser characters in *Limbo* are divided personalities who, in denying "Nature's joke"—ambivalence—become "character types" rather than fully realized human beings. Only when two or more of them are juxtaposed is the complexity of a Martine, or his female counterpart, Ooda, possible. The most explicit example of this split in the book is found in Martine's remarks about Theo and Helder: "I'm *both* of you, both of you rolled up in one, the neatest little packaging job in history! Yes, I'm Helder, and I'm Theo too—the gangster and the baby, the demon activist and the cherubic passivist, the leader and the follower. . . . But you two, you're *less* than human. Because each of you has denied his doubleness. . . Between the two of you you'd make a human being . . ." (370).

Similar hyphenations exist for combinations of other characters:

for instance, Theo, Jerry, and Tom add up to Rambo; Irene-Neen to Ooda; and Ubu-Helder-Vishinu to Don Thurman. These hyphenations are complemented in *Limbo* by the false opposition of "Siamese twins." The Mandunji Island is pretty much like the IMMOB society, and the differences between the Inland Strip and the East Union are mainly "semantic." The leader of the Pro-Pro party, Theo, and that of the Anti-Pros, Tom, are two spectacular types of psychic masochists, and the frigid Irene gets as little sexual pleasure as the promiscuous Neen. If the sick elements in *Limbo* tend to be equalized, they conform to Bergler's theory of the "basic neurosis," in which all neurotics are treated as victims of *one* neurosis, originating exclusively in the "oral phase" of a child's development. Thus if masochism equals impotence equals criminosis among the characters in Wolfe's novel, it is no wonder that their EMSIAC, IMMOB, and Mandunga are also thematically equated.

Wolfe's economic use of character, as well as his divisions and equations of types, has a direct relationship with the main concern of *Limbo:* the "joke." The specific kind of "joke" found in "mark i" is, according to Martine, an "extended pun," whose main characteristic falls under the category of "condensation" (as described, for one, in Freud's *Wit and Its Relation to the Unconscious*). The relationship of one character to another, of one society to another in *Limbo,* involves an economic tendency like condensation—the technique of wit concerned with word division, double meanings, and the formation of mixed words, all of which create puns through the splitting or juxtaposing of words (as Martine is created through the splitting and juxtaposing of the other characters). The central meaning of *Limbo,* then, comes full circle: the "hero" who was "born of a joke," who wrote a "dirty joke" in his journal, who found all humanitarian programs a "joke," is himself a "joke"; he is redeemed only because he learns to laugh at himself instead of "humorously revelling in pain" (400).

The pun, however, remains the central structural feature of Wolfe's novel. The very title of the book is a kind of a pun, as the emphasis of its meaning can be placed either on "limbo," a state between heaven and hell, or on "limbo-0"—the absence of limbs. The language of the novel, mouthed by Martine, is a catalogue of puns itself: "Oms do not make the man," "Russian bear never reigns but it paws," "passive-fier," "peeping-tometry, that's a branch of optometry," and so forth. Even the names of the characters suggest the techniques of wit, most notably with the association in *Limbo* of Martine and "martyr." Similarly, Don Thurman is a condensation of "Don(')t Hur(t)man," Helder of "Held (H)er" or "(T)he (E)lder," Mandunga of "man" and "dung," Teddy Gorman of "Gor(ed-)man," Tom from "loboTOMy," Neen of a compendium of negatives in many languages ("Nyet," "Nein," "No"), and IMMOB from "immobile." [8]

Finally, there is some typographical playfulness in *Limbo* which reflects the thematic importance of the "joke." The most striking are the giant "NO" (88) and "YES" (411), each occupying a full page in the midst of the narrative. (Together, they add up to "Noyes," Martine's mother's maiden name.) Likewise, the novel contains little drawings and doodles which often take the form of visual puns. Such frivolity, however, is thematically justified in so highly structured a novel. For evidence of Wolfe's attention to form, we need only compare *Limbo* to the anarchy of A. E. van Vogt's *The World Of Null-A* (1948), which is mentioned in Wolfe's "Author's Notes and Warnings." In using a work of science fiction to create a well-made novel, Wolfe stands again with such figures as H. G. Wells, George Orwell, and Aldous Huxley.

IX Limbo *and Beyond*

In its own way, Wolfe's *Limbo* may be as difficult a book as James Joyce's *Ulysses*. The latter imposes difficulties of form on a relatively simple narrative, while *Limbo* uses a simple form—the science-fiction, antiutopian novel—to discuss very complex theoretical material. Consequently, the preceding analysis is to be considered a skeleton key and not a complete explication of the novel.

Limbo must be considered, at the very least, Wolfe's most prototypic work. While he has not, since that novel, used the science-fiction form, his later novels are very much indebted to Bergler; and most often a protagonist with a special ability to verbalize his own masochism is set in opposition to a woman who practices a spectacular form of neurotic sexuality. As such, later characters are similar to the Amps, in that they participate in voluntary (if unconscious) self-maiming. Martine is found again in Gordon Rengs, Paul Teleki, David Justin, Hoyt Fairless, and Robert Garmes; Neen in Taffy, Connie, and Penelope; Ooda in Miss Shoshana, Frana Sherwood, and Donaji. Stylistically, the pun remains fundamental to Wolfe's work (as does the significance of laughter), although the emphasis on cannibalistic imagery is heightened. Such flash-backs, moreover, as the events of October 18, 1972, continue to retain a certain aloofness from the narrative.

Limbo remains a problematic (and critically unnoticed) novel in spite of its brilliance, in spite of promising reviews, and in spite of mass publication on both sides of the Atlantic. Although many of the political ideas in the novel will not stand up to the test of the 1970's, the fault in the past probably lay less with Wolfe than with his publishers and audience. The American paperback edition, for instance, had a tasteless cover destined to be unnoticed in the rather overwhelming pulp science-fiction sections of paperback bookstores. *Limbo*'s sales no doubt also suffered from its traditionally antithetical (in its genre) combination of science fiction and "heavy" theoretical material. Thus, many readers attracted by the adventure may have been repelled by the very demanding and difficult "essays" concerned with scientific and political ideas.

In this study the emphasis has been on the influence of Bergler because the psychoanalytic ideas in *Limbo* are not so explicit as the source material borrowed, for instance, from Norbert Wiener or Dostoevsky. Furthermore, psychic masochism is the most crucial element in Wolfe's antiutopia; and an understanding of the neurosis remains a point of reference for the complete unraveling of Wolfe's *Limbo*.

CHAPTER 4

Between Two Masterworks

I *Beyond* Limbo

AFTER the publication of his antiutopian novel, Wolfe wrote two short books before turning once more to a work of grander scope and magnitude: his study of Leon Trotsky entitled *The Great Prince Died* (1959). The short books, like *Limbo,* are intentional parodies of popular literary forms: *The Late Risers* (1954—reprinted as *Everything Happens at Night* in 1963) is a burlesque of Damon Runyon's stories of Broadway; and *In Deep* (1957) satirizes the thriller.

If the two books written in the mid-1950's are shorter and less ambitious than the masterworks which preceded and followed them, it is partly because both *The Late Risers* and *In Deep* were compressed by Wolfe's editors before their hardcover issue. Random House bought the *ideas* for both books as a package before either was completed. But, prior to the publication of the earlier book, Random House sold the reprint (paperback) rights to New American Library, and this new publisher insisted on limiting both books to eighty thousand words. The completed manuscript of *The Late Risers,* however, ran close to one hundred and fifteen thousand words. Because of the word-limiting clause in New American Library's contract, Wolfe's editors were forced to reduce the manuscript to ninety-five thousand words—after a compromise was reached. According to Wolfe, the compression seriously damaged or omitted some crucial passages clearly establishing the elements of parody in the novel. A similar fate awaited *In Deep,* even though Wolfe had left Random House after the appearance of *The Late Risers.* His new publisher, Knopf, was still tied to the New American Library contract; thus, the original manuscript of *In Deep,* which was one hundred and seventy-five thousand words, had to be cut by the editors to one hundred and twenty-five thousand words. Even then, the reprint publishers refused to print it; and, after writing off their investment as a loss, they eventually sold their rights to another paperback house.

Nevertheless, *In Deep* remains Wolfe's best short novel to date. Perhaps because of the cutting, the thriller in its published form is concisely constructed and lacks the tangential asides so typical of Wolfe's frequently overburdened work. Much of the writing represents Wolfe at his best (as a craftsman, at least); and, in particular, the skin-diving sections are probably among the most excellent to be found in fiction dealing with underwater life. In the context of Wolfe's own career, moreover, the novel anticipates many of the political themes which are worked out more elaborately in *The Great Prince Died*, while looking back with equal favor to the ideas and themes of *Limbo*. *In Deep*, as we shall see, is a true link between Wolfe's two masterworks as well as an exciting novel in its own right. Its success may be compared to its less satisfying predecessor, *The Late Risers*, which is more concerned with the interests expressed in *Really the Blues* than with political thought. (For this reason, the Broadway novel is discussed, more appropriately, in the chapter entitled "*Really the Blues* Reconsidered.")

II *The Plot*

The "story" of *In Deep*, like that of *Limbo*, occupies a number of psychically overlapping time intervals and settings. The bulk of the narrative occurs in the present (probably 1950) and is set in the Florida Keys and in Cuba (an island Wolfe had visited seven or eight times, and which he considered making his home before he was offered a job in Hollywood). Preceding the present are certain events, recalled in a lengthy flashback, which had occurred in the Pacific during World War II (the early 1940's.) Going further back into the past, other episodes in the novel are set in Spain during the Spanish Civil War (mid- to late 1930's) and, simultaneously, in Cuba. Finally, there are descriptions of the hero's adolescence in New Bedford during the Depression (early 1930's) and several brief glimpses of his early childhood, the marriage of his parents, and even a few details about his remarkable grandfather.

Turning first to the present, we find an extremely involved narrative that parodies elements frequently found in the thriller or novel of intrigue: the "amateur" hero who investigates the "organization" that killed his best friend; the spectacularly attractive girl friend who provides clues, "red herrings," and who eventually "proves" herself by deliberately receiving a bullet intended for the hero; the master criminal who is adept in the use of disguises and who manipulates the baser members of his "gang"; the "professional" investigator who tries to discourage the "amateur" hero because he wants to catch the master criminal himself; the lengthy chase and inevitable confrontation of the "amateur" and the master criminal. Moreover, Wolfe makes good use of the thriller's low-life settings (brothels, distilleries, carnivals) and of its characteristically well-spaced clues (the mysterious words of the dying friend, torn newspaper clippings and letters, purchased information and "leads").

The action begins in Key West, where hero Robert Heixas Garmes is in the "shark liver business." The oceanographer is susceptible to "drunkenness of the deep seas," a dangerous and even lethal form of intoxication caused by an excess of nitrogen in the blood of those who skin dive. Garmes's partner and friend, "Barto" Bartolome Caro, manages their four boats while waiting to complete a secret mission begun, we are informed, thirteen years before in Spain. As the first chapter of the novel concludes, Barto has just learned that the individual he has been seeking for so many years is in Havana. As he prepares to leave Key West, several characters are introduced who gain significance when the action continues in Cuba. At this point of the narrative, they function to bring the name Michael Brod to the attention of Garmes. The hero slowly discovers that the mysterious Brod had killed Barto's father in Spain, that he had attempted to kill Barto there as well, and that it is he whom Barto so obsessively hunts.

The first character to mention Brod is Professor Owen Brooke, a sociologist who studies Afro-Cuban ceremonial music and who, we later learn, uses Havana's Sociedad por la Música Afro-Cubana (SOMAC) as a contact with Brod, for whom he runs errands. Wolfe is quite merciless in his conception of the professor, who is represented as that kind of academic who takes all "jokes" seriously and who is thus responsible for the Brods of the world. Owen Brooke, whose name is a synthesis of the two most famous British World War I poets (Wilfred *Owen* and Rupert *Brooke*) continues in the tradition of *The Late Risers*' Professor

Vanderbilt Bohlen (discussed in a following chapter), whose name is a composite of two notoriously unscrupulous millionaires (the American Vanderbilts and the German Bohlens, one of the names of the Krupp family). Both professors record "authentic" tribal music, which is performed for them by those "authentic" blacks who are really interested in auditions and bookings. Wolfe's satire of the academic has been seen before in the section of *Limbo* dealing with the Moral Equivalents University and is found again in his more sensitive treatment of David, the university student who is murdered in *The Great Prince Died.*

A second character who speaks obliquely to Garmes in Florida about Barto's affairs is Vincent Caprio, who turns out to be *Major* Vincent Caprio, a member of the CIA assigned to the Brod case. From him, we eventually learn that Brod is a member of the GPU (the Soviet secret police). The two "institution men" are the novel's "professionals": both believe they are motivated solely by politics rather than by personal (or unconscious) impulse. Thus, they both operate through elaborate, well-constructed "plans" in which they attempt to "anticipate" all factors. So far, they have "anticipated" each other so well that they are in a perpetual stalemate: neither can make a move the other cannot foresee (rather like the Inland Strip and East Union in *Limbo*). Barto and Garmes, who represent the unpredictable forces, are at once courted by the "professionals" (in the hope that they can break the deadlock) and rebuffed by them (precisely because they cannot be "anticipated").

Nelson Boyar, an interesting peripheral character, stands in the same relationship to Caprio as Owen Brooke does to Brod. The CIA's errand boy, however, is not an academic; he is an alcoholic novelist who had written a number of proletarian novels in the 1930's. His most recent book, however, is a war novel entitled *The Determined Tigers* whose plot and title are obviously meant to suggest Irwin Shaw's *The Young Lions* (1948), but other evidence in *In Deep* also associates Brod with Ernest Hemingway. While Brooke criticizes *The Determined Tigers* as a "sellout to the reactionaries," Brod (in the last phase of the thriller) dismisses both the war novel and the earlier works as a mere "smokescreen" under which the "professionals"—who have little use for "slogans"—operate. Like Brooke, Wolfe implies, Boyar created the need for both Caprio and Brod by exerting the influence of his "slogans" on society.

Connie Overton is Boyar's well-built mistress. It is soon established, however, that her real lover is Garmes, who gives her sexual "tests" rather than minks and yachts. These "tests" are similar in type to that which Martine gave Neen in *Limbo:* during and after the sexual act, Garmes criticizes Connie's tendency to assume the leading role and exposes her concealed frigidity. Her sexual incapacity, Garmes argues, is partially traceable to her voluntary preference for the wealthy novelist rather than for the man she loves. At the same time, the oceanographer questions his own motives in choosing an unresponsive woman for a lover. (Because he needs support for his myth of woman-the-denier?) Here we find one of the applications of the novel's title: Garmes's relationship with Connie is *deeper* (more meaningful in terms of Garmes's past) than is at first apparent.

On the eve of Barto's departure, and after the above-mentioned characters have made their appearances, Garmes enters his friend's house and finds him with a knife in his back. Barto's murderer is, of course, the elusive Brod. Before Barto dies, he asks Garmes to find his little sister, Luz, who has been missing since the civil war in Spain. His last words contain a clue to Luz's whereabouts: "casa milagro"—the House of Miracles. With little other information and with both the CIA and the GPU closely behind him, Garmes immediately leaves for Havana, where the second phase of the present begins.

In Cuba, where Garmes discovers that he is really "in deep," more information about Brod is revealed. The agent's role during the war in Spain, as told by Barto in his last letter, is strikingly similar to that of his counterpart, George Bass, in *The Great Prince Died*. Both were Stalinists whose job it was to purge their own ranks of those militia men who questioned Stalinist policy, as did Barto's father, Barto, and Paul in Wolfe's novel about Trotsky. Thirteen years later, however, it is the *Stalinists* who are being liquidated by the *new* centralists in the Kremlin; and thus, like Bass, Brod discovers that he is suddenly out of favor. Knowing that his recall is imminent, Brod steals a document vital to the interests of the CIA with which he hopes to strengthen his position in the Kremlin and perhaps avoid execution. An agent representing the Kremlin's interest, Avelino, remains near Brod to see that he does not defect with the document. Meanwhile, another of Brod's men—Coolio, a black bongo player and addict—has the promise of a reward if he helps the Stalinist escape and sell the document. When Garmes enters the picture, Brod still has not decided whether to go "home" with Avelino or to disappear with Coolio. Eventually, he is influenced by Garmes, who decides midway through the novel to work with Caprio and the CIA.

But first, Garmes tries to pursue Brod unaided, except for the services of a Cuban ironically named "Benjie" Benjamino Francisco (Benjamin Franklin), who works at the same time for Brod and for Caprio. Benjie directs Garmes to the House of Miracles, a brothel where Brod's schizophrenic girl friend, Natividad, is employed. The girl is totally disoriented, but eventually, with her unwitting help, Garmes manages to catch up with Brod. It is then that Garmes discovers *why* he had been chasing the agent and why the agent had allowed himself to be caught: each man was drawn to his "mirror image." Despite their political differences, Brod and Garmes look alike; they have similar family backgrounds and interests; and they possess similar internal drives. As soon as he acknowledges that Brod is his "twin," Garmes can guess accurately what the agent's plans are. Just as the oceanographer is attracted by an underwater death, by the "drunkenness of the deep seas," Brod is attracted to the bullet waiting for him in the Kremlin, and he has arranged things in such a way to ensure the success of Avelino's mission. Moreover, he has even forfeited the document that might save his life. In the last pages of the novel, we learn that Coolio, then in the hands of the CIA, has the papers (which contain a list of the CIA agents working in the Kremlin).

Before Brod departs, he tells Garmes that Natividad is really Barto's lost sister, Luz. The girl's story is similar in conception to Martine's theory of the "sins of the sons" in *Limbo,* in which Wolfe suggests that environment (and parents) may not be the final influence on the formation of a child's character. As a Marxist, however, Brod is forced to believe that the perfect environment will create the perfect man. But years before, he was deeply shaken by the discovery that little Luz was retarded, even though her parents were—before the war in Spain—well indoctrinated. After Luz was orphaned, Brod placed her with some Mexican

Communists, but not even that "perfect" home (in Stalinist terms) could correct the girl's deficiency. Finally, in desperation, Brod gave way to "the secret conviction that his own phallus has magical powers that can uproot mountains and turn day into night" (264). While he raped her, Luz had an epileptic seizure which she equated with the highest pleasure. Thereafter, even though Brod was never to touch her again, she continued to "love" him and worked in a brothel in the hope of repeating her early experience.

The novel's conclusion occurs after Garmes and Brod have recognized their similarities and even—because of their encounter—*exchanged* certain superficial character traits (as though the reflection were to take the place of the reflected, something Mezz tried to achieve—musically—in *Really the Blues*). Garmes is now the "professional," the cool one; Brod is the manic "amateur," who dives "too deeply" and without doctrinaire rationalizations. Nevertheless, the agent manages to elude Caprio and to slip aboard the ship bound for Russia. The less astute Owen Brooke and Coolio, however, fall into the hands of the CIA, the latter after wounding both Natividad-Luz and her opposite number, Connie, and after being wounded in turn by Garmes. Finally, there is the characteristic reconciliation of the lovers, Garmes and Connie, who plan to return to Key West with a new partner, Benjie.

III *Theme*

The reader of *Limbo* is familiar with many of the principal ideas and themes suggested by the thriller. In Wolfe's third novel, we again find the struggle between two powers (the CIA and the GPU) whose differences are primarily "semantic"; the "jokers" (Marx, followed by his disciples, Brooke and Boyar) whose theories are institutionalized; the "butts" (Brod and Caprio) who will take drastic steps to validate these theories (even the rape of a schizophrenic child); the rebels (Barto and Garmes) whom the institutions can neither avoid nor take into account; and, of course, the "jokes" themselves (especially in this novel, the battle between look-alikes) which only the hero can appreciate.

Moreover, there are also shades of Martine in the character of Garmes. Like the lobotomist, the oceanographer is a "psychic masochist" who experiences a therapeutic recall of painful childhood memories during his adventures and who is "cured" during the narrative. For Garmes, the recollections of the past come about as visions experienced during deep-water dives. (The skin-diving sections of *In Deep* are written in italics and precede each chapter of the novel.) In these sequences, or preludes, we learn about Garmes's parents and about his life in the navy.

The racially mixed Annie Florence Heixas and the "Fifth Avenue" aristocrat-in-disgrace, Charlie Garmes, had the kind of marriage which, Wolfe suggests, would confirm a child's most monstrous fantasies. The parents of Robert Garmes were characterized by their complete reversal of traditional roles: Charlie was a passive idler, delicate, disgusted by sex. His inability to so much as stand up was legend. Annie, by contrast, was inherently masculine: she did a man's work on their boat; and, despite hardship, she was the sole support of her son and her husband. Young Robert, like his mother, was repelled by his father, although secretly attracted at the same time by Charlie's passivity. As Martine would have recognized, Robert's anger was "pseudo-aggressive"; it concealed a deeply "masochistic" belief that his *mother* had been Charlie's real "murderer" and that the same fate awaited him. When Robert was seventeen, after years of pretending to take his mother's part, Charlie suddenly and unexpectedly took his son's "joke" seriously. While Robert was taunting him, Charlie tried to commit suicide by diving overboard and by swimming into the boat's propeller. He imagined that it was "snake-bristling Annie Florence Heixas . . . he saw there in the propeller. Arms going like a windmill"(235). Although his father was badly mauled, Robert shared his triumph: the graphic "proof" that Annie was a murderous "Ogress."

As an adult, Robert Garmes compulsively repeats the conditions surrounding his father's "accident." In the navy, Garmes rebels against a well-meaning but bookish intelligence officer who reminds him of his father, until, inevitably, the officer, too, has his face chewed off in the water—by a stray *American* bomb. (Here Wolfe also attacks military "consistency" which refuses to acknowledge such "ambivalent" and "absurd" factors as bombers that roam off course.)

After the war, Garmes again chooses a boat for his "home," which gives him ample opportunity to seek propellers—and death—in deep-water dives. In his dreams, he even associates Connie with his mother: both typify the mythic "bad" woman that he and his father need. Finally, Garmes uses the novel's central adventure to re-create his own family situation. He begins the "chase" in reaction against two *strangers* who remind him of his father—Caprio and Professor Brooke. Eventually, he allies himself with Caprio because Brod, he realizes, "brought to mind my mother, hands on hips, full of energy and impatient, thinking ahead." And, in the course of the narrative, Garmes once more manages to get in serious trouble with Brod—on a *boat*. It is only when the oceanographer discovers that Brod is more like himself than his mother that the "myth" he had cherished since childhood is shattered. At the novel's conclusion, Garmes can "forgive" his mother—by accepting Connie as simply another troubled being—and his father—by laughing at Caprio instead of attacking him, and so achieve "health."

Characteristically for Wolfe, the hero's private "neurosis" is meant to be associated with the social "neurosis" that threatens populations. Brod, too, had a strong mother and a weak father; consequently, he, too, secretly seeks death—perhaps at the expense of civilization. Neither the agent nor his country, then, can be labeled the "bad" one. Human behavior, Garmes admits, is more complex than can be depicted in "a chase story in the movies," in which two men "run at top speed, without any slackening, and the virtuous man catches the unvirtuous one because he can, with his virtue, run faster"(174). In reality, Garmes continues, "you don't have good and bad sifted in two separate packages" (174); thus, the chaser and the chased tend to resemble each other.

In *In Deep,* then, Wolfe continues his examination of the dynamic aspects of character, the changeable forces in the personality which contain our true hope for social and psychological rebirth. Garmes's "cure," like Martine's, proves once again the credo of Mezz in *Really the Blues:* there is "joy" for the "twice-born man" who survives his ordeal, although now "joy" is thought of as psychic health, and the "ordeal" is the revelation of unconscious thought and memories. Wolfe was to persist with his psychoanalytic approach in his second masterwork, *The Great Prince Died,* in which the themes of the thriller are again applied to contemporary history.

CHAPTER 5

The Great Prince Died

I *Beyond* In Deep

AFTER writing his two parodies of popular literary forms—*The Late Risers* (1954), a satire of Damon Runyon's Broadway tales; and *In Deep* (1957), a caricature of the thriller—Wolfe turned once more to a serious work. *The Great Prince Died* (1959) is Wolfe's most overtly political novel, a book continuing in the tradition of *Limbo* and fulfilling the promise of *In Deep.*

Wolfe's "Great Prince" is Leon Trotsky, the former leader of the Russian Revolution who dies in Mexico, murdered by an agent of his ideological and political enemy, Joseph Stalin. While the main concern of the book centers around Trotsky's personal anxieties during the last weeks of his life, the larger issues have a striking resemblance to those in *Limbo.* The antagonism of Trotsky and Stalin, for instance, is similar to that of Martine and Helder. Like the lobotomist in Wolfe's earlier novel, Trotsky wrote books on permanent revolution in which his argument for the use of violent "means" to achieve a good "end" might be construed as an unconscious "joke." Stalin's (and even Trotsky's) "misreading" of the "joke" is used to justify a kind of "voluntary amputation" within the Communist party, which is characterized by successive purges culminating in the notorious Moscow Trials and in the assassination of Trotsky. As troublesome "limbs" of the party are cut off, Stalin, like Helder, consolidates his power and authority, inevitably subverting the Communist ideal for his own purposes. Unlike *Limbo,* however, *The Great Prince* ends with a qualified pessimism; for Stalin and the forces of evil win, while Trotsky dies with his more "humanitarian" cause; but the lowly peons, who have nothing to "amputate," are last seen laughing.

While the examination of recent history in *The Great Prince Died* strengthens the political thesis first dealt with in *Limbo*'s antiutopia, it also continues to explore the nature of contemporary man in society. Wolfe again questions the validity of the political formula as well as the motives of those who support it. Furthermore, he still supports Freud's argument in *Civilization and Its Discontents* that society and instinctual happiness are inimical by postulating in *The Great Prince* that the restrictions imposed by a political program *must* fail if concessions are not made to man's natural need for immediate satisfaction. Fundamentally, Wolfe once more insists that man must decide whether any "utopia," or even the "comfortable" society of the present, is worth the freedom and happiness he is obliged to sacrifice (or amputate). The emphasis is on man as a *dynamic* being, who is responsible for his condition and who is *free* to make the choice between a healthy or a neurotic society.

II *Toward* The Great Prince Died

In print, at least, Wolfe's association with the Trotskyities appears to have begun as early as 1934, when his name was listed among the contributors to a May Day Greeting in a New York-based Trotskyite organ, *The Militant.*[1] At the time, Wolfe was still a student at Yale, where he joined a small nucleus of Trotskyites who had disassociated themselves from the more numerous Stalinists. Encouraged by his new friends, Wolfe published a number of political articles about the Spanish Civil War in *The Militant* and in another Trotskyite newspaper called *The New International.*

After leaving New Haven and Yale in 1937, young Wolfe was sent to work for Leon Trotsky in Mexico as a secretary and as a member of his security staff. In another version, however, Wolfe says he went to Mexico at the request of the John Dewey Commission of Inquiry, which was then preparing for the hearings concerning the Moscow Trials, to act as the liaison between the commission and the press. During the eight months he remained in Mexico, according to the notes appendixed to *The Great Prince,* he sensed "some profound and unacknowledged crisis in Trotsky's life" although he admits that "at twenty-one I was less than an astute observer of politics and personalities"(384). His early impressions of Trotsky continued to develop in the years after Trotsky's death in August, 1940; but until the mid-1950's, he did not have the "emotional distance" to turn his Mexican experiences into literature. About this time, he wrote a one-hour television play for Philco Goodyear based on Trotsky's murder and called *The Assassin.* It was presented "live" on February 20, 1955. Meanwhile, he turned the teleplay into a full-length play and used it as the basis for the novel which was published as *The Great Prince Died* in 1959. Thereafter, he wrote a screenplay adaptation for independent producer Josef Shaftel; reportedly this version is not being used for Joseph Losey's film about Trotsky.

The fictionalized accounts of the last months of Trotsky's life dramatize events occurring more than eight years after the aged revolutionary had been exiled from Stalinist Russia. While attempting to find asylum in the capitals of Europe, he had been hounded successively through Turkey, France, and Norway. Finally, his American friends had obtained a Mexican visa for him and his wife; and, in an atmosphere of classic intrigue, they had arrived in Coyoacán, a suburb of Mexico City, in January, 1937. For the first time since his banishment from Russia, Trotsky was free from internment or restriction. The Mexican Revolution was then at its climax; some land had been distributed among the peasants; and industry was being nationalized. The political climate induced the Mexican government to treat Trotsky as a guest of the country. Diego Rivera, the Mexican painter, had invited the Trotskys to live in his house, and there Trotsky fortified himself against the extended arm of the GPU—Stalin's secret police.

The Trotskyites previously had been Stalin's only effective opposition; and Trotsky, continuing to be Stalin's loudest critic, had been the GPU's prime target. In the period immediately before his assassination—the interval covered in *The Great Prince Died* —Trotsky worked on his biography of Stalin, exposing the purges, the Moscow Trials, the Stalin-Hitler pact, the sellout in Spain. But the effect of his activites was minimal—his supporters were silenced by both the Moscow purges and internal confusion caused by Trotsky's frequent shifts of attitude. His four children and four of his grandchildren were dead; only his second wife and a fifth child were left.

The background of the "real" Trotsky, however, is not identical with the hero of Wolfe's novel. The latter has only one wife and one living child, and the date of his assassination is moved back to February, 1939, in order to simplify the sequence of events. These and other changes are documented and explained in the appendix to *The Great Prince,* in which an attempt is made to justify the differences between history and fiction. (Even so, in *The Prophet Outcast,* [437], Isaac Deutscher—Trotsky's biographer—complains about Wolfe's factual inaccuracies.) Nevertheless, in an effort to prevent "misreadings" of his intentional distortions of Trotsky's life, Wolfe changed the name of his hero to Victor Rostov. Significantly, the substituted name is taken from Tolstoy's *War and Peace,* in which the Rostovs are a noble Moscow family-in-decline. A familiar name in Russian literature thus replaced a towering name in Russian history, emphasizing, it would seem, Wolfe's commitment to esthetics rather than to political "truth." Similarly, the title of *The Great Prince* is drawn from a literary source: Stendhal's *The Charterhouse of Parma,* a novel concerned with political intrigues in the nineteenth century. Wolfe's literary concerns in his political novel are frequently evident, not only in "factual inaccuracies," but in the extensive use of parable, the dramatic tempo of the narrative, the heightened imagery, and the structured opposition of personalities, ideas, and events.

III *The Plot*

Wolfe's unique, indeed idiosyncratic, approach to the fictionalization of Trotsky-Rostov's last days is summarized in his notes: "It occurred to me that [Trotsky's] final tensions must have centered on Kronstadt as much as on any one supra-personal thing, and that, accordingly, a meaningful telling of the man's story would have to dig back to the island massacre of 1921 as it moved ahead to the crash of the Alpine ice axe that ended his life almost two decades later. The present book became possible when I saw that the GPU-sponsored blow could be taken, and in a sense *had* to be taken, as a last spasm of the corpse of Kronstadt" (384).

Characteristically, the book combines the techniques of essay and narrative. The essays—in excerpts from the writings of Rostov and the Rostovites, magazine articles, ideological discussions, and "David Justin's Glosses" appendixed to the book—are primarily concerned with the consequences of the Kronstadt uprising. These are supplemented by the inclusion of a number of parables relating to the 1921 massacre.

The narrative of *The Great Prince,* however, begins after Victor and Marisha Rostov are settled into their Coyoacán house, rented from a famous Mexican sculptor. The high wall surrounding the house prevents external assault but imprisons the inhabitants. The GPU agents in Mexico have arsenals at their disposal, but Rostov, now occupying a defensive position, attacks only with his pen. Concerned with larger questions, he is unable to oppose even the daily nibbling of the Mexican Communist newspapers, which create the emotional atmosphere that precipitates the eventual assassination. Within the walls, the Rostovs are aided by three followers: Paul Teleki, bodyguard; David Justin, American translator; and Emma Sholes, secretary. From a position immediately outside the walls, the omnipresent peon, Diosdado, watches the maneuverings of General Ortega, chief of the Mexican secret police assigned to protect Rostov, and the GPU agents: George Bass, the organizer; Ramon, the "heavy"; and Candida, who is currently out of favor. She is the bait that insures the cooperation of her son, Jacques-Masson, who has been ordered by the GPU to become Emma Sholes's lover and thereby gain access to the Rostov's house. George Bass periodically reinforces Jacques's commitment by threatening to send Candida to Moscow and, presumably, to her death.

The action that follows is a development of conflicts which originate before the opening of *The Great Prince*. Each character is motivated by personal as well as by political involvements. But the greater part of the novel takes the form of a discussion about the Kronstadt uprising of 1921. This "original sin"—the symbolic "wall"—culminates, according to Wolfe, in the cat-and-mouse relationship of the GPU and the Rostovites in 1939.

While the GPU is organizing Plan A (a massive attack on the Coyoacán household) and Plan B (the murder of Rostov by a lone assassin), the Rostovites venture beyond their walls for a day's outing, which at first appears to be a deceptively uneventful picnic. But the occasion serves as a temporary release of tension for all, a final nerve-twitching before the "spasm" to come. Masson, overwrought, slaughters butterflies by the hundreds in a fit of rage; and, similarly, Paul shoots vultures without obvious provocation. Meanwhile, George Bass has seized the moment to incite a "spontaneous" peon attack on the Rostovites. Ramon tells the local farmers that Rostov is a foreigner who has come to seize their recently acquired land; and the peons, infused with the spirit of their own revolution, march upon the picknickers. Rostov saves the party with a fiery speech in broken Spanish, declaring his comradeship with the Mexican rebels.

After the Rostovites are again safely behind their walls, George Bass proceeds with Plan A—an armed attack on the house by GPU agents, Spanish Stalinists, and Mexican sympathizers. An evening is chosen when David Justin is defending the door (Paul is far less vulnerable) and when Jacques-Masson is house guest. After Paul returns drunk and unalert from an evening in town, Jacques compels David to open the door for the attackers. A shower of bullets is fired into the Rostovs' bedroom, but Victor and Marisha are saved by hiding under their bed. David, however, is killed by the attackers before he can accuse Jacques of being an agent. Thus, all of Rostov's previous reservations about Jacques's loyalty are dispelled when he is seen "fighting" the attackers.

In the interval between Plan A and Plan B, pressures increase. The president of Mexico, coerced by American concern, urges Ortega to arrest the allusive GPU. After Hitler's invasion of Czechoslovakia, the Kremlin orders the GPU to hasten the assassination of Rostov and the destruction of his writings about the consequences of the Stalin-Hitler pact. At the same time, antagonism among the Rostovites reaches the point of mutual renunciation: Rostov asks Paul to leave Coyoacán, and Emma plans to return to the United States with Jacques. In the background, the demands of the peons for more and more land gain strength.

George Bass precipitates Plan B with a decoy—the arrest of seven Mexicans who attacked the Rostovs' house. From their knowledge of GPU tactics, the Rostovites presume that Plan B will be unlike Plan A, but they blind themselves to Jacques's increasingly obvious inconsistencies. In fact, not until the day of the second attack does Jacques discover the role he has been assigned —he is to be the assassin of Rostov. Believing his mission suicidal, Jacques hypnotically chooses an ax as his weapon; entering Rostov's study, he delivers the death blow from behind. But Rostov does not die instantly; his scream brings Paul to the scene, who prevents Jacques's escape.

Rostov, on his deathbed, acknowledges the weakness of his position about Kronstadt. But neither this concession nor his death can alter the chain of events originating in the 1921 rebellion. The GPU, for instance, is subjected to an internal purge. George Bass is supplanted by his steely comrade, Ramon, and sent to Moscow with Candida. Jacques is wanted in the Kremlin as well, but he evades his prearranged "escape," preferring life in Mexican prison to death at the hands of the GPU. The Rostovites are now totally disbanded: David is dead, Emma has a breakdown, and Paul retires from politics and civilization by settling in a primitive Mexican village. In addition, General Ortega has been thoroughly disillusioned and has left without the moral conviction to deal with peon demands, while Diosdado is last seen as the victim of bureaucracy, entangled in a meaningless system of documentation. The only "victor" is Stalin, the archfiend of our time, who does not hesitate to use the most inhuman means of achieving his ruthless ends.

IV *"What to Do About Kronstadts"*

There are three central problems posed by *The Great Prince Died:* "What to do about Kronstadts"; "What to do about Stalins"; and "Who makes history?" Typically for Wolfe, these issues are not entirely resolved in the novel; but, as we shall see, a spectrum of familiar solutions for them is tested and rejected. As in *Limbo,* and in *In Deep,* moreover, the political problems are complicated by the unconscious and infantile wishes which motivate even the political man.

The Kronstadt affair, conceived by Wolfe as the obsessive scar on Rostov's conscience, actually occurred in 1921, three years after Russia and Germany had signed the Treaty of Brest-Litovsk. The Bolsheviks found themselves at the head of a country devastated by civil war, a food and fuel shortage, industrial stagnation, full-scale Allied invasion, and open conflict among political leaders. In attempting to rescue Russia's crippled economy, the Bolsheviks instituted the policy of "War Communism," which involved nationalization of industry, appropriation of food from the peasant farmers, obligatory industrial labor for the bourgeois, and special privileges for members of the party. In an appendix entitled "David Justin's Glosses on Kronstadt," Wolfe synopsizes his version of the events that followed. The War Communism policy provoked considerable unrest, which was climaxed in February, 1921, by a strike of the hungry workers of Petrograd. By March 1, the unrest had spread among sixteen thousand Kronstadt sailors, who had formerly been the pride of the revolution. The sailors still declared their loyalty to the Communist party but demanded basic libertarian rights: freedom of speech, land rights for peasants, equal rations, individual small-scale production, abolition of political bureaus. Lenin and Trotsky, who promptly labeled the uprising a mutiny, insisted that it was inspired by the White Guard although the evidence was to the contrary. On March 7, Communist military units (led by Rostov in *The Great Prince*) fired the first shots at Kronstadt, although up to this time the sailors had not harmed one Communist. On March 17, the troops entered the garrison and slaughtered the sailors. Hundreds more became victims of reprisals. Ironically, on the day before the final attack, March 16, the party congress had voted to discontinue War Communism in favor of the New Economic Policy—which included measures originally demanded by the Kronstadt sailors.

In *The Great Prince*, the Rostovites are haunted by their uneasy justification of the Kronstadt affair and by its connection with the moral validity of their political lives. Why did the uprising occur? Throughout the first half of the novel, Victor Rostov remains committed to the theory that the rebellion was motivated by White Guard interventionists. According to David Justin's "Glosses," however, the rebels rejected White Guard aid offered at the time of the rising, and, furthermore, the Bolsheviks know about their refusal. Clearly, the White Guard theory was a face-saving gesture originally adopted by Rostov and his followers to turn attention from more embarrassing causes. When Rostov is provoked by Paul during the picnic, he claims that the Kronstadt rebels had to be silenced lest they destroy the revolution. The masses had been promised land and freedom in 1917, but time was needed to stabilize the revolution before the promises could be met. According to Rostov, the rebels could have been appeased only at their own expense—immediate satisfaction for the masses would have destroyed the Bolsheviks and everything they were trying to attain.

This interpretation fails to convince Rostov's followers and critics. David in particular refuses to accept a political precept to "explain" Kronstadt. If the rebels had been unreasonable in seeing no further than their stomachs, the Bolsheviks had been worse in seeing no further than their formulas. Moreover, the rebels had been annihilated, not merely silenced; such violence goes beyond ideologies. (The difference between healthy and neurotic aggression has been outlined in Bergler's table, reprinted in *Limbo.* David intuitively recognizes that violence in excess to its provocation is "unhealthy.") Expressing the thoughts that Rostov cannot vocalize, David prefers to think of the causes of the uprising in neurological terms: both Rostov and the rebels had been compelled by a "spasm," a "tick," a "muscle contraction" (as was Martine, the neurologist in *Limbo,* when he disobeyed EMSIAC). Man's neurological system prompts his hungers—for freedom as well as for food, power, violence, or for the sheer act of incorporation realized in *The Great Princes*'s cannibalistic imagery. Midway through the novel, Rostov senses the connection between hunger, neurology, and his role in the Kronstadt uprising: "They marched on Kronstadt not to kill. (In the face of danger some animals eat their young.) Rather to preserve. (Yet some animals eat their offspring as a tic, only because their jaws will not stop working)" (105).

Before Rostov's assassination, he realizes that neurology alone does not explain the Kronstadt affair, at least as far as his own actions were concerned. The October Revolution was indeed created by a "spasm" of the masses; but its leaders, or those who became the leaders of its new government, were impelled by psychoanalytic motives. In a letter to his fiancée, David analyzes the unconscious causes behind Rostov's early politics. When he was fourteen, young Rostov organized strikes among the peasants working for his father. He must have conceived of the world as divided between stern fathers and oppressed but rebellious sons, and this conception had influenced his personal and political actions for the rest of his life. In his youth, Rostov became a Narodnik (the Russian term for Populist—the radical intelligentsia who supported a peasant revolution), attracted by their romantic and quasi-anarchic belief in "openness, fluidity, individual will over groups"—a reaction against the oppressive rigidity of his father.

Eventually, Rostov turned to Marxism, but according to David, he remained the anarchic-individualist at heart; Marxism was an unconscious excuse for Rostov to rebel against a much sterner father than his own—Lenin. For the next fourteen years, until the Revolution in 1917, he attacked Lenin and the Bolsheviks compulsively, primarily for their "bone dryness and steel hardness." In 1917 came a sudden collapse. The rebel attained his revolution;

the son became a father. Once in power, Rostov not only embraced Lenin and the Bolsheviks, he also became far "sterner" and "dryer" than they ever had been. Finally, at Kronstadt, a new generation of rebel-sons attacked the Bolshevik-fathers with the same quasi-anarchic demands previously raised by the Narodniks. Rostov had to destroy the Kronstadt rebels because they were a reminder of his own youth.

The tension between the rebel-son and the patriarch father has been treated previously in embryonic form in *Limbo*. Martine, the archetypal rebel, had killed his dying son, Tom, because the boy caricatured his father's weakness. But, while Martine was halfway redeemed because his act could be called euthanasia and because he had compensation in a good son, Rambo, Rostov embodies a father-son dilemma which is not so easily justified after *Limbo*. In *The Great Prince*, the political world is again treated as a macrocosm of the family situation in which both "father" and "son" must fight each other to "disprove" their own secret desire for passivity. The young Rostov who organizes strikes against his father, then, was participating in an act of "pseudo-aggression" similar in motivation to the older Rostov's murder of the Kronstadt rebels "for their own good."

The struggle for power between generations is seen by Wolfe, who follows Bergler's suggestion, as an externalized defense aganst unconscious infantile desires; therefore, the "hards and drys" and "opens and fluids" turn out to be very much alike—indeed, they are "Siamese twins" capable of instant merger. In this sense, "What to do about Kronstadts" is the same problem as "What to do about sons." Wolfe contends that it is the father's (or the government's) responsibility to learn how to deal with the often justifiable "spasms" of their rebel-sons—and to do so without allowing infantile fears and desires to interfere.

Each character in *The Great Prince* represents a different solution for this problem, although Wolfe does not allow any easy answer to emerge. Many of the attempted solutions, in fact, are presented as totally impractical simply because, in the course of the novel, the characters representing them die. These include Rostov, David, and the GPU agents (destined to be executed in Moscow after the action of the novel has been completed), George Bass and Candida. Rostov's solution was applied during the actual Kronstadt uprising, when he chose to destroy the rebel-sons. But the personal consequences were heavy: after "proving" his toughness so spectacularly in 1921, his aggressive instincts were satiated and the forces of *inertia* could then dominate his ego instead. (The same seesawing of the life-preserving and life-defeating instincts characterized Martine in *Limbo* and Garmes in *In Deep.*)

Immediately after the Kronstadt reprisals, Rostov exchanged an active military command for an administrative post. He passively allowed Stalin to undermine his remaining power until his banishment from the Communist party and Russia. In exile, he did not take the minimal precautions for self-defense, although he knew his assassination was imminent. Paul is continually disturbed by indications of Rostov's death wish at Coyoacán: the former revolutionary leader refuses to hire more than one bodyguard or to stock weapons. But beyond the psychological damage arising from Rostov's solution lie distressing social, moral, and political consequences. The Kronstadt uprising marked the beginning of the end of Bolshevik integrity; the unnecessary violence of the Communists (which, as David points out, could easily have been avoided) set a precedent for future totalitarianism and dictatorship in Russia. Moreover, the annihilation of the rebels, whose cause was just if shortsighted, was a betrayal of the principles behind the October Revolution. Finally, violence against the rebelsons did not stop them; for, as Paul points out, "once you let a little Kronstadt happen, it reproduces like rabbits" (207).

General Ortega, who is treated in some respects as Rostov's alter ego, demonstrates the evils of Rostov's solution even when it is applied with intelligence and sympathy. Ortega's "Kronstadt" originated in the Mexican Revolution, whose analogies to the Russian Revolution are emphasized in the novel. The peons, like the Kronstadt rebels, were impatient with guarantees after their revolution had been achieved: they wanted an immediate and universal distribution of land. Many were able, in fact, to acquire land when some of the larger estates were divided and dispersed. In *The Great Prince Died,* the Mexican government has the best of intentions; and, unlike the Bolshevik leaders, the president really is concerned with the fate of the peons.

General Ortega, for instance, retired to his estate after the revolution to establish an experimental farm which would improve the peon's primitive agriculture—a necessity for the survival of the country. At the time of Rostov's assassination, rebel peons are demanding the distribution of Ortega's land in spite of its beneficent function. Moreover, Ortega is greatly disturbed by the realization that his personal desires influence his solution—he very much wants to be a gentleman-farmer. Eventually, however, he enlists the president's aid in putting a stop to peon demands. Although he does not go to the extreme of annihilation, Ortega's conscience is troubled by the similarity of his actions and Rostov's at Kronstadt.

The solutions of the two young men, David Justin and Paul Teleki, are complicated by their dual function in the novel: David is the intellectual; Paul the "man of action"—but both also participate in a father-son conflict with Rostov. The younger Rostovites nag their leader with embarrassing questions about Kronstadt and are unsatisfied—like the peons and the Kronstadt rebels before them—with the lack of an *immediate* answer (although a real explanation would destroy the Rostovite cause). Rostov again handles his rebel "sons" with a sternness characteristic of the 1921 uprising—he tells them to leave Coyoacán.

Even though David is a university man (a type frequently attacked in Wolfe's work), he has one redeeming, if negative, quality: he is able to recognize the pointlessness of his own position at Coyoacán. Shortly before the picnic, Rostov asks him why he came to Mexico. University life, David answers, was too far removed from world events. Lecture halls confine rather than expand the student's knowledge of the masses. Rostov finds the weakness of David's position: "Claustrophobia is a bad reason for turning to public life. The streets are not a gay place. They are for people who have no other place to go"(45). In the notes that follow the novel, Wolfe continues his argument with the intellectual who suddenly discovers the streets and thinks them romantic (an argument heard before in *In Deep*): "No special merit attaches to being a beast of burden, a hand of factory or field. . . . Fringe-dwellers live out their lives in cramp and blight and that is their total story"(393).

Even worse, for Wolfe, is the tendency of left-liberal intellectuals to see oppression only where it conforms to their "consistent" vision of political life. In the 1950's, for instance, Algeria and the Congo upset them, although they ignored, according to Wolfe, the atrocities practiced in Communist China when it seemed to offer promises of a utopia. Shortly before his death, in the novel, David decides to return to the university where "comfort can be a program too—not the worst" (177–78). All other programs he has encountered have failed to help the oppressed; furthermore, his student battle against conformity—and fathers—proves also to be pointless. Wolfe suggests that an intellectual must retire from politics, where he can only cause damage (David is too unsuspecting to keep the GPU agents from opening the door at Coyoacán and attempting to assassinate Rostov) and die meaninglessly.

Paul Teleki (the name is derived from the Aristotelian term, *entelechy*, meaning "actuality") came from Bulgarian proletariat stock. Like Rostov, Paul rebelled against his environment and home in his early school days. A "man of action," Paul later went from street brawls and strikes to the battlefields of Spain and then Mexico in an attempt to fight the oppressors of the working class. By the time of Rostov's assassination, however, Paul realizes that his puny militant gestures have in no way helped the oppressed or solved the riddle of Kronstadt. The death of Rostov, who had become Paul's second father, somehow calms his high-key political aggressiveness (because the fight against fathers is finished?); and he ultimately finds his solution in retirement from politics and civilization.

In the last pages of the novel, Paul—typically for a Wolfean hero—is about to settle in a primitive, preindustrial Mexican village where he might "adjust to a life filled with acres instead of continents, hours instead of eras. . . . Accommodate himself to the small and immediate, live within the confines of his eyes' and ears' minute by minute data" (352). Immediately before he leaves Coyoacán, Paul eats an hallucinogenic mushroom given to him by his Indian friend, Donaji. Some Indians find a solution by concentrating on the "pictures inside," but Donaji's father is killed by an automobile while walking though the city under the influence of the hallucinogenic drug. If Rostov is assassinated because he is too busy with the "pictures outside," his political formulas which exclude human psychology, the Indians are also unaware of the dangers of their formula: "Too many nice pictures to look at inside and you do not see the situation coming" (352).

The GPU agents, George Bass, Ramon, and Candida represent

the cog-in-the-wheel solution to the Kronstadt problem: they will do anything for the good of their cause if ordered from above—including torture, murder, betrayal, and suicide (all of which are personally reprehensible to them). Moreover, they are aware of the Kronstadt-in-reverse condition of their occupation. Their ranks are periodically purged by their dictatorial superiors in Moscow to enforce the secrecy of their operations or to replace agents whose political conditioning has become obsolete when changes in Soviet policy occur. The Rostovites respect the agents because of the extent of their commitment (although this commitment is enforced in the Kremlin with hostages). One of the arguments in the novel, in fact, concerns the kind of commitment necessary in political life.

The terms "professional," "amateur," and "dilettante" are frequently thrown around in connection with the various solutions to the Kronstadt problem (as they were in *In Deep*). Bass, for instance, is considered a true "professional" because of his single-minded efficiency, but Ortega is accused of "dilettantism" when, after "the joy of a thoughtless hitting out at the fathers"(132) during the Mexican Revolution, he retired to his farm, reluctantly returning to public life only at the request of the president. But these distinctions are obscured in the face of "Kronstadts," where, according to Wolfe, the only "professional" is "the man nailed down in a slave-labour gang—the most fully 'committed' man of our time"(395).

V *"What to Do About Stalins"*

The Kronstadt uprising is presented not only as the moral test of our times in *The Great Prince Died;* but as the preamble to the major atrocities which have occurred since—from the Moscow purges to the Auschwitz gas chambers. Wolfe takes this unorthodox view in part from Leonard Schapiro's hard-line study, *The Origin of the Communist Autocracy* (1955) which traces the demise of all Bolshevik opposition to the 1921 rebellion. The uprising, like Theo's voluntary amputation in *Limbo,* created an atmosphere of solidarity within the party that enabled Lenin to take strong measures to silence all dissenting voices; and this power led, in turn, to the first party purges. At the same time, Stalin's position was strengthened within the party when he attacked the unpopular reprisals, endorsed by Trotsky, against the Kronstadt rebels. The slow tarnishing of Trotsky's intentions eventually allowed Stalin to control the party and Russia.

The novel picks up this argument in a critique of Rostov's career published by a French Socialist periodical. Using the book's characteristic images of a cannibalism, it contends that "Bolshevism's hunger for the flesh of its own corpus" (68) began at Kronstadt and not, as Rostov had been insisting in articles written at Coyoacán, in Stalin's trials and purges. Rostov's answer is specious at best: perhaps Kronstadt did create the precedent for Stalin's brand of dictatorship, but that it did was the fault of the rebels, not of the Bolsheviks. The Socialist organ continues by reminding Rostov that in 1904 he had predicted that Leninism would lead to the worst form of centralism—Stalinism.

The progression from a well-intentioned revolutionary party to the evils of autocratic centralism is outlined in a parable during the Rostovites' picnic. A brief excursion takes the sightseers to the terraced pyramids built by the Toltec Indians eons before. Rostov is most impressed by the towering sun pyramid and discusses its history for the picnickers in terms of an analogy to the Bolshevik cause. The theocratic priests (Lenin, Rostov) of the Indians (Russian masses) considered themselves the descendants of the sun (Marxist ideology). They incited the peons to build pyramids (the October Revolution); then they mounted "the pyramids to elude the refuse who have no kin in the sky" (84). While the theocrats on top were blinded by the sun (Marxist formulas), chaos reigned below—food was scarce and crops failed (the conditions in Russia under War Communism). The pyramid cities were eventually destroyed by agricultural fatigue, by rebel peons (Kronstadts), and by invasions by the "Dog People" (German and Allied forces on Russian soil before the signing of the Brest-Litovsk Treaty).

Meanwhile, instead of inventing plows for the peons, the theocrats were perfecting mathematical systems (political formulas) in honour of the "shining Oneness" (centralism) of the sun above. Why? "The craving of the fragmented! The One Party universe—a dream of multiple personalities!" (85). The theocrats were internally terrified of becoming as "scattered" as the peons below. They finally were toppled by law of monoliths: "Those who rise to the apex can't see the base; . . . the base will rise up one day, not seen until the last minute, and destroy the apex" (84–85). Stalin, however, was more astute than the Toltec theocrats—he was not blinded by Marxism; he continued to look downward to the masses at the base and to control them. He would unhesitatingly annihilate another Kronstadt before rebellion could occur again.

Why had Stalin been able to override the law of monoliths? The younger Rostovites, Paul and David, feel that the means-ends theory, advanced by Rostov in his book about permanent revolution, backfired at Kronstadt. In 1921, the Bolsheviks—like *Limbo's* Helder, before his leadership was established—were prepared to use the most drastic means (the liquidation of their own people at Kronstadt) to achieve their end, a centralized government. In the novel, Stalin represents a literal application of this idea, now repugnant to Rostov; the "drastic means" even include the assassination of their original theorizer. By the time of Rostov's assassination, Stalin's control has spread beyond Russia, and the precedent established at Kronstadt has also reached even further.

The best example of this spread, in *The Great Prince,* is related to the Spanish Civil War, where Paul, Jacques-Masson, and the GPU agents served their apprenticeships as revolutionaries. Wolfe accepts the "special" interpretation of Stalin's ambitions in Spain found in General Walter Krivitsky's *In Stalin's Secret Service* (1939) and in Jesus Hernandez' *I Was a Minister of Stalin* (1953). Stalin realized that the leftist position was hopeless in Spain, and in the mid-1930's he was convinced that Hitler would some day conquer Europe. In order to placate the Nazis and promote a Soviet-German pact, Stalin secretly decided to "sacrifice" Spain (and more than seventy thousand men) to the Fascists. In his exposé of Stalin, being written at Coyoacán in 1939, Rostov claims that Stalin's policy of appeasement in Spain allowed Hitler to believe he could safely invade Czechoslovakia; and, consequently, Wolfe implies, the horrors of World War II would occur (though after the action of the novel is completed).

In the novel, Stalinist objectives, both within and without Russia, are usually accomplished directly or indirectly through the GPU. This terrorist organization operates through a system of checks and counterchecks. Every Plan A is backed by Plan B; in back of every member is a hostage whose life depends on the success of the plans. Every supervisor is spied upon by his underlings. No one working for the GPU is ever allowed knowledge of an entire operation—the participants of Plan A know nothing of Plan B, and often not even that they are part of a plan. In short, the GPU is a highly organized agency capable of the most skillfully arranged maneuverings to maintain those in power.

The history of this organization, moreover, is a microcosmic analogy of the consequences of centralism. Wolfe traces the origin of the GPU, again, back to the Kronstadt uprising. In 1921 Rostov gave the Cheka (the predecessor of the GPU) the order to carry out reprisals against Kronstadt, ironically giving the secret policemen an impetus which would still be active in 1939. The previous assassination of their own comrades "justifies" their assassination of their former leader, Rostov. The original Cheka, furthermore, had consisted of intellectuals and theorists; but in the novel they are replaced by men who, like George Bass, are statisticians, yet men with ideas. After the pact with Hitler, however, Bass in turn is succeeded by the end product of Stalinism—Ramon, a mindless tough from the waterfront of Barcelona.

In this context, it is significant that most of the agents in the novel have names connected with fish: George *Bass,* Candida *Baeza de Rivera.* The image no doubt is meant to be associated with a *school* of fish, in which individual fish thoughtlessly swim with the current until eaten by larger fish. Bass, for instance, a former taxicab driver from Philadelphia, obtained his position by marrying the sister of Stalin's friend. His ambition is to "look like the dullest, greyest Bass ever born; and, from the shadows, to make the dull and grey hop to his tune" (97). But a seemingly insignificant mannerism destroys his "greyness" and is symptomatic of a streak of impulsiveness which eventually spells his downfall: he calls attention to himself by continually playing with an object in his pocket—an optical glass, used to torture possible informants by a "concentration of too much sunshine" —a symbol of centralism in *The Great Prince.* Ramon connects Bass's mannerism with his disorderly attempt to raid the picnickers and the unsatisfactory outcome of Plan A, and reports both to headquarters in New York. As cunning as he is, Bass eventually falls out of favor because he is a degree less ruthless than his superiors—the larger fish—and in his kind of game the hungriest fish wins.

The connection between the GPU, centralism, and Kronstadt is again made in the form of a parable: the Sheridan Justice episode. The incident occurred in Spain at the time of the Moscow Trials, in which former comrades and party leaders who did not adhere to present policy were denounced and executed. Paul, like Barto in *In Deep,* was assigned to the American Abraham Lincoln battalion in Spain; and, when its commander was killed, he was voted acting commander. But the party, thinking only of its American propaganda, chose Sheridan Justice as the permanent company commander. Sheridan, a semiliterate "bottomdog Negro" from Alabama, had formerly worked in a paper-bag factory and had gone to Spain at the instigation of the party which promised to advance the cause of the "black proletariat" of America. Now, for the first time in his life, he was placed in a position of power; and, without any understanding of the consequences of his actions, he sent his men on suicidal missions. Finally, because of Sheridan's power-crazed fumbling, only six of his men remained alive—including Paul. The six mutinied against their commander and, despite Paul's objections, murdered him.[2] This action and the Moscow Trials were "the opposite sides of the same dirty joke" (192), according to Paul, because, like the centralists with whom they identified, the mutineers had shot not an enemy but a mere incompetent who "couldn't be held responsible for the political forces that had raised him, still blinking, to command level" (197).

As in Kronstadt, one purge soon led to another. The mutineers, like the rebels before them in 1921, had killed their comrade because they sensed that the Soviet cause was collapsing beneath them. (This impression was to prove correct with the signing of the Stalin-Hitler pact.) The Brigadiers in Spain knew they were being used, and they began to have "spasms" which impelled them to strike at the easiest targets. The mutineers were really trying to kill the crushing centralism proliferating from Moscow; now the centralists had to annihilate the mutineers—as Rostov had done once before.

George Bass and Candida, working for the GPU, were conducting these purges in the International Brigade at this time. After his death, Sheridan had become a party "hero," and all threats to his image had to be destroyed. Paul, who was obviously bothered by the injustice of Sheridan Justice's death, quickly fell into their hands. GPU methods of extracting a confession from Paul began with a sort of psychological "dismemberment": the centralists touched the most central nerve of the unconscious—the residue of infantile fear of the pre-Oedipal mother, who once seemed a muderess to her child and a far less dangerous figure than the pre-Oedipal father. Thus, Candida was threatening and abusive; George Bass was soothing and protective; but Paul withstood their re-creation of the infant's nightmare. When mental torture did not work, the agents resorted to physical torture. Ramon used George Bass's optical glass to burn off three of Paul's fingers, but he still refused to confess. The narrative continues with his deportation to Moscow, his experiences and escape from a labor camp, and his eventual meeting with Rostov in Mexico.

The war in Spain, GPU treachery, and Rostov's assassination are all instigated or determined by Stalin, who cannot be so easily murdered as Helder was in *Limbo*. Moreover, the problem of "What to do about Stalins" goes hand-in-hand with concern about who has the moral right to fight dictators. Rostov lost his right at Kronstadt; Ortega, when he retired to his farm after the Mexican Revolution and forgot his political obligations. The implication is, of course, that no one's hands are clean; in the end, it is a matter of a lesser evil fighting a greater one. Nevertheless, a number of solutions are tested in the novel. Rostov, ironically (considering his solution at Kronstadt and his theory of permanent revolution), tries to fight the Stalins through pacifism. At Coyoacán, his "death wish" becomes increasingly evident in his refusal to defend himself against GPU attacks. After Kronstadt, he is unable to consider a solution involving guns—guilt feelings about the 1921 uprising are too close to the surface to permit another slaughter. Instead, Rostov writes endless anti-Stalinist articles and books, hoping that exposure will somehow stop Soviet aggression through embarrassment. Rostov's own death, however, is a dramatic indication of the inadequacy of pacifism—as Wolfe had pointed out in *Limbo*—the first man with a gun can crush any pacifist gesture.

Paul represents those militant forces who wish to actively defend themselves against the onslaught of Stalins. At Coyoacán, he is continually fortifying the wall (a pervasive symbol in the novel), but he forgets its one weakness—the door. This breach in the wall, guarded by David, the guileless intellectual, permits the Stalinists, through sheer strength or cunning, to find a way in. After the assassination, Paul discovers a similar weakness in his primitive Mexican village that is surrounded by a "wall" of thick jungle. The Indians sell sarapes to businessmen in nearby cities, and one of the "businessmen" is GPU agent Jacques-Masson. According to Wolfe, there is no way to hide or protect oneself from Stalins: the apolitical man is as much a fool as the "man of action"—both can be easily crushed.

By the end of the narrative, Ortega has decided upon a vigorously offensive line (for others at least—he will retire again). His sense of dignity is outraged because Rostov was wounded from behind: "This is not a stylish game and there are no rules except to win. . . . Is the world run and altered by proud swords? Or by cowardly axes? . . . the question was answered. The evidence was in" (337). Any sense of morality or sportsmanship in the face of a Stalin is adolescent: "Those who use all means will win, those who reject some means will lose" (311). Rostov's weakness, as we have seen, is that he did not take his own "means-ends" theory as literally as a Stalin does. Wolfe suggests, ironically, that one must become a Stalin to effectively fight one.

The situation is summed up, characteristically, in the form of another parable. In the interval between Plan A and Plan B, George Bass sees a movie called *The Hardening Trees* (really *The Petrified Forest*). In it, the poet (Leslie Howard) is pitted against the gangster (Humphrey Bogart), and until the last minute the gun is far more formidable than the word. In the end, the gunman is destroyed only when *two* other gunmen appear. A Stalin not only uses millions of guns but far more insidious weapons also (propaganda, GPU tactics, pacts with Hitler); and his opponents will be as defenseless as the pacifist poet in the film until the weapons are equalized. Thus, *The Great Prince* refutes the solutions to the problem of evil traditionally found in novels in this century and before: good does not automatically win; poetry, metaphysics, hallucinogens, orgasm—all are useless, a "joke," in the face of Stalins, Hitlers, and H-bombs. Wolfe can only recommend that we somehow stop Stalins at the Kronstadts, their origin, before their political programs proliferate and annihilate us. At the same time, we must maintain a realistic view of the possibilities of victory and, through "healthy aggression," defend ourselves against oppressors.

VI *"Who Makes History"*

The power of a Rostov at Kronstadt, of Stalins, or of centralists in general depends upon a basic fallacy—the "greyness" of the masses. The peons have neither face nor name; all hints of personality are completely washed out; they are just—peons. The "grey" ones, not being individuals, have, of course, no rights; they exist only to satisfy the power cravings of Stalins and Hitlers. They may have occasional "spasms," but they do not consciously fight for freedom. (Yet, when on his deathbed Rostov is finally capable of seeing beyond this lie, he remembers the face and words of his friend Anastas Yiko, whose red beard was a vivid indication of color among the Kronstadt rebels.) *The Great Prince,* through narrative and image, insists that the peons do, in fact, have color, individuality, personal needs, and a desire to resist manipulation.

The centralists and GPU agents (gray steel and gray fish, as their names indicate), on the other hand, are deprived of color through their monomaniacal lust for control. They do not have half the spark and energy of the Kronstadt rebels, who were prepared to die rather than submit to the humiliation of "greyness." Diosdado, far from being the castrate that "greyness" implies, has eight children, while Rostov—the only other father in the novel—has one son who turned against him because of Kronstadt.

The "color" of the masses is represented allegorically in the episode concerning the striped girl. A few hours before the Coyoacán household is attacked in the course of Plan A, Paul visits a local vaudeville-burlesque show. One of the acts involves a peon, Oliviero, and a nude Aztec girl painted with bold red and yellow stripes. The striped girl remains expressionless while the peon tells a number of low-brow phallic and political jokes about his own virility and the impotence of the government. After the show, Paul sleeps with the girl and is amazed to discover that she will not accept money: she regards her body as treasured property which can be given but not sold. Her self-respect, the prerequisite of health for Wolfe, is found only among the peons in the novel, who have no Kronstadts on their conscience.

Wolfe stresses the individuality of the masses in order to attack, as in *Limbo,* political ideology per se, whether it be of the Right or of the Left. (Hitlers and Stalins are "just coming at the same idea from opposite directions" [148] like Helder and Vishinu in the futuristic novel). Political formulas, because they are based on a desire for "consistency," must reduce people to the lowest common denominator; they presuppose that the "masses," as a collective unit, really exist. The "masses," however, are merely an abstraction of separate and individual people who may be economically linked. Futhermore, the role of the "masses" in history is closely connected with the idea of the indispensability of their leaders. Would Kronstadt have occurred if Rostov and Lenin had been bookbinders instead of politicians? Before his assassination, Rostov answers yes—Kronstadts (and history) are inevitable. Their leaders merely swim with the tide of circumstance. But, as David and Paul point out, there were alternatives to Rostov's actions at Kronstadt which could have changed the course of events. Rostov could have sided, for instance, with the rebels. He was strong enough in those days to have exerted his influence on their behalf and could thus have prevented the slaughter. The argument rests on the question of whether history is the product of determinism or free will, and evidence in the novel abounds for the latter: the world is run by forceful individuals and individual forces.

These individuals are themselves determined, however, by their own "neurotic" needs. Jacques-Masson expresses this idea in simplistic terms: history, he says, is formulated by one's attachment to mothers and sex. And, indeed, as the reader of *Limbo*'s psychoanalytic material may realize, Jacques's secret anger and secret desire to be punished by his mother eventually erupts when the assassin kills with the ax (a reminder of his mother's "axe-edged" nose?), another attempt of a truly passive individual to complete "the job muffed in the nursery." His intended victim, then, was the fierce pre-Oedipal monster that Candida so forcefully represents—a female equivalent, for her son, of the Stalin who destroys in the name of the public good. Of course, Jacques only succeeds in murdering another haunted male—Rostov—because, Wolfe suggests in his antiutopia, such a symbolic return to the crib *must* be accompanied by misguided destruction.

In fact, the shadow of Candida darkens the soul of many characters in *The Great Prince,* although Wolfe does not discuss the influence of the pre-Oedipal mother as explicitly as in *Limbo* or *In Deep.* Nevertheless, an acquaintance with Berglerian psychology may permit the reader to infer that the problem between fathers and sons could never have become so acute if a fear of the mother had not preceded it. Presumably, the Rostovites cannot effectively oppose Stalin because they unconsciously do not differentiate between the Soviet leader and the fantasized "murdering" mother. Like Jacques, they can fight anything *but* the symbolic oppressor of their infancies because of a "masochistic" desire for torment. Even Rostov intuitively notes his ambivalent reaction to the centralists when he remarks, "things in this less either-or than both-and world [have] such a thirst to be impregnated with their own negations: dung can sprout roses" (104).

In short, the history-makers in *The Great Prince* are psychically "unhealthy" individuals, whose distorted visions have produced the dangerous and destructive twentieth-century situation. Rostov's erratic biography is outlined *twice* in the novel, each interpreting his political actions as a defense against neurotic or ambivalent wishes, expressed even on his deathbed: "Take axe . . . to butterflies" (323). In these last words, spoken while he is in a semicomatose state, is a summation of the conflict which had dominated his life: the man who secretly wanted to be a "butterfly"—something "soft," passive, and feminine—had frequently camouflaged his unacceptable wish by assuming the guise of an "axe"—a "hard," aggressive patriarch, the "supreme centralist" who could easily murder the masses at Kronstadt. Jacques's role in history, as we have noted, is similarly determined by his personal neurosis: punishing his mother by beating her proxy, Emma, is not enough; he must kill her in Rostov while pretending to "save" her from Stalin at the same time. (The assassin's behavior appears to follow Bergler's theory of three-layered neurotic symptom: the forbidden wish, the defense against the wish which is also forbidden, and the subsequent defense against the defense.) Whatever its "political" consequences, the murder seems to release Jacques from his terrible attachment to his mother: in the last pages of the book, he evades her "tyranny" by remaining in a Mexican prison instead of cooperating with the GPU-inspired escape plan.

The "healthy" individuals, by contrast, avoid the sickness of political life. Wolfe compares the tangled relationship of Jacques and Candida, Rostov and his father, with the ideal parent and child—the Indians, Donaji and her father. When Donaji's father dies, she is not overwhelmed by the essentially contradictory emotion called "grief" by Western society; such a display would be symptomatic of the paralyzing attachment typical of "neurotic" relationships. Instead, she is saddened but able to function normally, finishing her father's business and rearranging her own life, as her father would have wanted her to. He had never asked his daughter to conform to "civilized" conventions at the expense of her freedom. When, for example, it seemed that marriage would destroy her ambition to become a teacher, he recommended that she take a lover. Donaji, in return, had no reason to "punish" her father by rebelling against him, and he found no rebellion in her to crush.

Those whom the makers of history chose to ignore—the peon who desires a small piece of land rather than a continent; the Indian who wants two sarapes instead of one; the Kronstadt sailors who preferred immediate libertarian rights to a utopia they might never see—react to Stalins and Rostovs in two ways. They have a tension-releasing "spasm" in the form of a mutiny, a riot, or some sort of exercise "just to stretch their cramped muscles." ("And that," Wolfe adds, "though not always world-shaking, is fine, very fine" [398].) Or, more typically, they react to the muddle of government with *laughter.* The oppressed people who can experience, through laughter, a higher form of reality untouched by the restraints of society, had been discussed by Wolfe in *Really the Blues,* although in *Limbo,* he corrected this idea by noting the aggressive component in laughter, which the futuristic leaders found dangerous enough to forbid. Nevertheless, the peons laugh because politics is a "joke"—essentially absurd. In *The Great Prince,* the healthy chuckles of the masses are parabolically expressed during the picnic, when Rostov, who has been making grandiose comparisons between the pyramids of the Aztecs and the Soviet centralists, looks up to see a peon urinating from the heights of the pyramid walls. Thus, all walls, internal and external, built by theocrats and mothers, are burlesqued.

Diosdado, whose name means "little God," represents all the urinating peons overlooked by their formula-conscious governors.

His small adventures are cross-cut in the novel with the assassination narrative, and he is most frequently shown as taking advantage of the political situation in any way possible. His bravery and vitality always compare favorably with the humorless mania of the Rostovites and Stalinists. For instance, while the Rostovites concentrate on GPU tactics, Diosdado steals an automobile tire (from which he will make gauraches—sandals—for his large family) from under their noses. When the politicians are distracted by "the sun," the little man is quite capable of obtaining what he needs.

The final chapter of the book continues to demonstrate the absolute futility of offering even beneficent government aid to Diosdado. The Mexican bureaucrats institute social security for the peons and perform mass marriages so that the status of peon families can be determined. Diosdado, who has been with his "wife" for nine years, looks upon the ceremony as nothing more than a great festival, and he sells his marriage certificate for eighteen pesos minutes after it has been registered. Having accepted an immediate reward rather than postponing it for a social good, "all in his family, his duly certified family . . . were laughing with their heads back" (369). The "Great Prince" died, in the last analysis, for a "joke."

VII *The Fictionalization of History*

There are some special difficulties in assessing a novel that takes such an admittedly partisan view of a historical event that occurred within living memory. As pure literature, *The Great Prince Died* competes with *Limbo* as Wolfe's masterwork. As contemporary history, however, *The Great Prince* can be judged only by those of Wolfe's contemporaries who suffered—however remotely—the communal crush of the Alpine ax. It could be noted in passing, though, that as a political man Wolfe took a giant leap from A to B when he changed his allegiance from Trotsky's "Centralism" to Bergler's "One Neurosis."

Wolfe's Rostov is a "psychic masochist"—the mental disorder found again and again in all of Wolfe's heroes. Ironically, it is only Diosdado, the happy peon, who has a seemingly natural immunity to the psychoanalytic epidemic. Presumably, members of the dark races never experience "pseudo-aggressive" fathers or monstrous pre-Oedipal mothers, and thus they escape the burden of aristocratic pain. Wolfe's attitude toward Third World people harks back to his view of the "bellylaughing Negro" of *Really the Blues*, a view he tries to update in other novels, as we shall see in the next chapter of this study.

CHAPTER 6

Really the Blues Reconsidered

I *Beyond* The Great Prince Died

WITH the publication of *The Great Prince Died* in 1959, Wolfe appeared to have exhausted the overtly political interests which emerged in *Limbo*'s antagonism between the Inland Strip and the East Union, which were continued in the narrative complications of *In Deep*, and which were elaborately developed in the story of Trotsky-Rostov's assassination. To be sure, in Wolfe's next novel, *The Magic of Their Singing* (1963), an account of the "hipsters" in Greenwich Village is occasionally interrupted by references to the Israeli-Arab conflict, while *Come on Out, Daddy* (1963) briefly returns to the battlefields of Spain. But since *The Great Prince Died*, Wolfe has been primarily concerned—to date—with satire directed at the cults and shrines of nonpolitical America: "hip" ghetto blacks, Greenwich Village "beats," Hollywood's film and television industries, hallucinogenic drugs, Orgone therapy, Eric Berne's transactional analysis, swimming pools, public relations, and the generally warped values of American "fun culture" of the early 1960's.

By and large, Wolfe has continued to examine the hero whose "joke book" is taken seriously by the society he represents. In *The Late Risers* (1954), a book published immediately after *Limbo* and reprinted in 1963, hero Don Kiefer ghost-writes a syndicated gossip column, much of whose contents are based upon the "jokes" and deliberate falsifications submitted by agents and public-relations men. In *The Magic of Their Singing* (1961), Hoyt Fairliss is writing a dissertation for Harvard's Political Science Department which could eventually enable him to get a job in the State Department. His subject, however, has so little to do with the realities of politics that he privately calls it "*The Thepectwum of Neutwalith and Commitment in Miwwel Eatht Fowwin Powithy.*" Academicians, Hoyt suggests, make textbooks of nonsense; thus, one should speak about university business and requirements in the accents of a two-year-old.

Yet the idea of the "joke book" receives less attention in either of the above-mentioned novels than it did in *Limbo* or *The Great Prince* or than it would again in *Come on Out, Daddy.* The central concern of both *The Late Risers* and *The Magic of Their Singing* is, rather, to expose and to satirize the mid-century mythology which evolved around such New York-based "fringe groups" as "Beatniks," Broadway types, and premilitant blacks. The two "fringe-group" books, despite their many structural and thematic similarities to Wolfe's archetypal novel, *Limbo,* seem to have a more covert relationship with *Really the Blues,* if only to renounce it. Strangely enough, each of the two books were published soon after the appearance of a more significant work: *The Late Risers,* two years after *Limbo; The Magic of Their Singing,* two years after *The Great Prince.* It is possible to conjecture that Wolfe's publishing schedule may have been influenced by a private ritual of exorcism, in which he was compelled, between "serious" books, to return to the subject of his early biography if only to reject what he wrote there. Is *The Blues,* then, Wolfe's own Kronstadt, an early "joke book" he is frequently moved to correct? We have noted that he dismissed the ideas mouthed by Mezz in *The Blues* in two essays written around 1949. As an artistic experience, however, the book about jazz remains far more satisfying than do either of the "fringe-group" books, which may be considered the least successful of Wolfe's novels. Possibly, Wolfe's failure to outdo *The Blues* represents his own inability—as an old member of several "fringe groups" himself—to come to terms, as an artist, with his own intellectual ideas on the subject.

Wolfe's two essays on black culture—"Uncle Remus and the Malevolent Rabbit" and "Ecstatic in Blackface," the first published in *Commentary,* the second in *Modern Review,* and both in Sartre's *Les Temps Modernes*—are portions of an unpublished and uncompleted book called "The Congo on Main Street." Wolfe was unable to find a publisher for the manuscript in 1949, when books about racial tensions appeared infrequently. (However, the published portions did attract the attention of the militant black, Franz Fanon, in *Black Skin, White Masks* [1967].) In *The Late Risers* Wolfe was able to rework many of the themes used in his non-fiction study in his conception of the black character called

"Movement." To a lesser extent, History Jones, the black in *The Magic,* was similarly evolved. Most striking for the reader of *Really the Blues* is the great difference in characterization between the black friends of Mezz and their more "ambivalent" counterparts in the two later novels. In these books, Wolfe examines the racism and secret orthodoxy of those who would "cross the color line."

II The Late Risers

The publishing history of Wolfe's second novel, *The Late Risers,* is similar to that of his third, *In Deep.* As we have noted in an earlier chapter, Random House gave Wolfe a contract for both books, then sold the paperback rights to a reprint publisher who limited the unfinished books to eighty thousand words each. When *The Late Risers* was completed, however, its length was almost twice as long as was stipulated. Eventually, the editors cut the book to ninety-five thousand words, seriously damaging the "takeoff on the happy ending," which appears in the published version as an orthodox, rather sentimental happy ending. As several reviewers have noted, the tone of this unauthorized ending is inconsistent with the rest of the novel and remains its weakest section. In 1963, *The Late Risers* was reprinted in paperback form under a new title, *Everything Happens at Night.*

Risers is Wolfe's deliberate parody of the Damon Runyon stories. The novel is populated with the "guys" and "dolls" who hang around Broadway during the hours when "normal" people are home in the suburbs, asleep. These late risers, who do not get out of bed until after noon, are as obsessed with time as with Times Square, a characteristic reflected by the structure of the book whose chapter divisions each represent a given segment of time: "1:00 pm—2:35 pm," "2:35 pm—4:00 pm," and so on. As the action progresses to the novel's concluding chapter, called "6:00 am—6:30 am" (the hour when the Broadway prowlers retire), the pace becomes manic as individual deadlines approach. One is often reminded of the British film *The Small World of Sammy Lee,* whose hero (played by Anthony Newley) spends an evening racing from friend to friend, trying to borrow or raise money before a debt becomes due. As Wolfe was to note again in *In Deep,* all such Sammys are really chasing what is "missing" in themselves.

During the single afternoon and evening described in *Risers*, a number of "practical jokes" occur, which to some extent are related to the old Times Building, whose illuminated headlines can be read from a distance on Broadway. Three items attract the attention of the regulars on that day: "UPSTATE FOREST FIRES BLANKET NEW YORK WITH RECORD SMOG" (5), "LOCAL TAX BUREAU MEN REPORTED UNDER FIRE IN EXPANDING SENATE CORRUPTION PROBE" (7), "BIFF JORDAN, HOLLYWOOD COWBOY STAR, RUMORED IN TOWN" (7). The first provides an appropriate symbol, a "mask" for the city which conceals various activities and their motivations. The second affects Connie Marci, a corrupt Bureau of Internal Revenue Service investigator, who secretly "shakes down" prostitutes Lovis Doreen, Francine and Jinni, and Betsy Bugbee. The third item, concerning Biff—a cowboy who hides an allergy to horses when he is before the camera—touches off the master "joke" of the evening as frantic preparations are made for the star's arrival.

Most of these preparations fall on the shoulders of Mort Robell ("More Trouble"), a press agent who threatens to "cut off his big toe" if columnist Benny O. Bliss does not print an item concerning Mort's client, Lovis Doreen. Meanwhile, despite the agent's desperate search for a way to pay his debts, he is forced to turn his attention to Biff's needs: "reefers" (marihuana) purchased from the black called Movement; contact with Connie Marci who is arranging "the tunnel deal," an elaborate form of tax evasion for Biff; and "a blond, not platinum." It seems that the star, who is actually only semipotent, suffers from migraine if he does not have a woman within a forty-eight-hour period. As the pressures of the day mount, Mort is left with little choice other than to find a pretext for sending the "virgin" Betsy Bugbee to Biff's hotel room. When Betsy discovers the cowboy's intentions, however, she protects herself with jujitsu and then runs off to her secret lover, Movement. Only Connie Marci knows that "virgin" Betsy prostitutes herself to out-of-town businessmen while playing the "innocent" on Times Square.

Biff's headache, which begins with Betsy's departure, worsens in the second part of the "joke," ostensibly designed to keep the star away from women. The "jokers" are Danny Atlas, the owner of a novelty store called "Fun, Inc."; Leo Carney, the manufacturer of novelty ties inscribed with slogans; and Gil Lazarro, Leo's office manager, who retired in his youth after losing his leg (*Limbo*-like) in the war. The three pay Solly, who punches out the headlines for the Times Building, to falsify a bulletin stating that the M-U-K film executives want Biff to play God in a biblical epic. The "jokers" then send Biff—through Mort—the supposed phone number of the executive's room, but this number is really the phone company's test for the busy signal. While Biff spends the night trying to contact the producers, the M-U-K executives, who really *are* secretly meeting in New York, see the bulletin and decide to take it seriously. However, they, too, are given the number for the busy signal. Eventually each exasperated party gives up the other as "missing."

The theme of the "missing person" is continued in narrative material involving Leo Carney, whose obsession is tracing missing heirs. For the past months, he has been trying to locate a Minnie Kropotkin, whose surname suggests the philosopher of anarchism, Prince Peter Kropotkin. Mrs. Kropotkin's husband had a secret bank account of twenty-seven thousand dollars which had never been claimed. Her son, it seems, was Guy Bromley, Biff's sometime homosexual companion, who had recently dressed like Marie Antoinette and hanged himself in Central Park. Toward the end of the night, Leo finds Mrs. Kropotkin in the Bronx. When he informs her of her good fortune, however, she is enraged at the notion of the years of poverty unnecessarily endured because of her late husband's "joke."

Interwoven with the above material are episodes concerning Wolfe's two mouthpieces, the alcoholic human-interest writer and would-be novelist, Howard Blakely, and Benny O. Bliss's ghost writer, Don Kiefer. (The latter is in part an autobiographical representation of Wolfe as the ghost writer for columnist Billy Rose.) Both writers are themselves "missing persons" in the sense that they "lose" the artist within them while doing the "hack" work for which they do not even earn by-lines. Kiefer—the "ghost"—also acknowledges his own "prostitution"—the compromise of his talents for money; and it is this compromise that attracts him to Broadway's most notorious prostitute, Frana Sherwood. In contrast to Betsy Bugbee, it turns out, Frana is actually a *virgin* around whom a mythology has grown and been precipitated by her secretly impotent Broadway clients. At the novel's conclusion, Frana and Don (and Howard) leave Broadway for the greener pastures of New Mexico, where they will raise Tennessee walking horses and children.

Standing somewhat apart from the other "jokers" is a serious joker, Professor Augustus Wedemeyer, a student of Max Weber, who dies in the course of the novel. While trying to reconcile the teachings of Freud and Marx, he contracts leukemia and finds death threatening before he can finish his book. He then asks Don and Movement to help keep him alive by "magic." Wearing a primitive death mask, he insists that his friends bring an authentic voodoo doctor to his deathbed. But such doctors, too, are "missing" in New York, and Movement is forced to impersonate a witch doctor for the Professor, who dies knowing that he has been "conned."

The confidence trick is the single motif which runs through all of the episodes and vignettes intercut in *Risers,* and it is this same theme that we find so frequently treated in Damon Runyon's stories of Broadway, as, for instance, the crone who poses as an aristocrat in "Madame La Gimp," the professional husband killer who seems to be a doting wife in "Lonely Heart," and the tough "gorill" who secretly fears his wife in "Blood Pressure." But equally influential in the conception of Wolfe's novel is Melville's *The Confidence Man,* whose subtitle—*His Masquerade* is slightly altered for use again in *Risers,* which is subtitled *Their Masquerade.* Movement, who had memorized Melville's novel, tells his friends that Melville's confidence man is really "Uncle Sam." The American is a "missing person" because he has no prefabricated identity, as do most Europeans. "So far America [has not] been able to generate any single, recognizable image of an American" (192). This lack of a ready persona, of a sense of self, has forced the American—as represented in *The Risers*—to assume a number of "masks" and disguises, to turn to "jokes," "magic," and confidence tricks, all of which are substitutes for "authenticity." The choice we are offered is between "confidence" —a healthy knowledge of self—and "con," the only activity possible for "missing persons."

The narrative portions of the Broadway novel are concerned with some rather spectacular confidence tricks as performed in Times Square, an area self-consciously devoted to the most deceptive of tricks, the illusions of happiness[1] and grandeur: illusions fostered by "fun" stores, instantaneous bulletins on the Times

Building, and a night life which appeals to those who, Wolfe suggests, wish they could alter the course of the sun. The trick of the day, as we have noted, is that precipitated by Biff's arrival. This "joke" is supplemented by the tax-evasion schemes of *Con*nie Marci (whose name itself is suggestive); the "tricks" of prostitutes which pass for authentic sex; the "tricks" of virgins who may be prostitutes and of prostitutes who may be virgins; the "confidence game" of public relations, in which columnists print falsified items deliberately submitted by unscrupulous agents; and a large number of minor "jokes," too numerous to be mentioned, which contribute to the total atmosphere of manic duplicity.

The confidence trick and the practical joke, like *Limbo*'s joke-taken-seriously, both have tentacles reaching back to the crib, to the time when the infant believed that anything was possible and that *he* could control it all. Reality is rejected by the "joker" "who feels cramped in a logic-spined world, has to explode it to give himself elbow room" (192). This notion that anything can be changed into its opposite, even night and day, or that "miracles" and "magic" are commonplace, allows some "magicians" in the novel to dream of "remaking" themselves: besides Gil's amputated leg, there is Danny Altas' nose operation, Guy Bromley's transvestism, and Frana's father's removal of warts. (Here we have an obvious link with *Limbo*'s voluntary amputation and with *Come on Out, Daddy*'s "Image changing.") At the same time, others try to "remake" themselves—indirectly—by "remaking" some aspect of the external world. Leo Carney, Broadway's "Magic Gesture boy," gives gifts to strangers (to strangers who perhaps do not want them) in lieu of being changed by a similar "miracle" himself. And Benny O. Bliss quotes his mother in his column, hoping that this "magic" will prevent her from dying.

Perhaps the most complex "magician" in the novel is Professor Wedemeyer, a character who is closer in conception to *In Deep*'s Michael Brod than to such typically effete academics as the "chase" novel's Professor Brooke or *Riser*'s Vanderbilt Bohlen (a folk musicologist who taught Movement how to play the bongos, then "discovered" the blacks' "authentic" musical heritage). Professor Wedemeyer had throughout his life taken offense at the Dionysian—the moments of excess which transcend the rational, particularly when applied to "language in its charismic functions" (111). Being a Marxist, "his whole search was for some materialistic explanation of . . . mysteries" (112), mysteries which nevertheless fired his imagination. But his efforts to "cage in concept" the dark magic of the jungles have little validity, he thinks, unless he can shed light on the master trickster, death. (Like the Californians in *Come on Out, Daddy,* death threatens the Professor's infantile sense of immortality and his secret belief in self-determination.)

On his deathbed, Professor Wedemeyer—perhaps taking the advice of Dylan Thomas' poem, "Do Not Go Gentle into That Good Night"—reacts to his prognosis with rage instead of resignation and is determined to fight death through the magical incantations of voodoo. But Don speculates that even this last request may be a kind of confidence trick directed at "magic" itself: "Maybe, in addition to being dead serious, this man, with a final blast of outrage against his own request, was poking fun at it, mocking as he demanded and beseeched" (124). The Professor dies at midnight, still fighting to see a reality "boiled down to consistency! To one single, homogeneous molecule" (239). Immediately before the Marxist draws his last breath, Don whispers a spontaneous eulogy: "Your life had a busyness, goldmines of contradictions—this was what made so many of us love you, for being so all the way human, such a concentrated picture of ourselves! That a man's story has no end, only convolutions—that was your story" (240).

In a variety of ways, a refusal to acknowledge or a mockery of death is characteristic of many of the Broadway "regulars." Mort, whose name means "death" in French, has a phobic fear of death; Benny O. Bliss tries "magic" to save his mother from galloping cancer; Guy Bromley commits suicide—in fancy dress; Frana's mother is outraged by the "asymmetry" of death during a near-fatal car accident; and Don Kiefer wears an undertaker's suit in bitterness after hearing—erroneously—that Frana is a prostitute. The "ghost," furthermore, does not believe in "magic" or in "jokes." As Frana points out during their reconciliation, Don's mask of hardness is as unhealthy as the excesses of Professor Wedemeyer or of the owners of "Fun, Inc."; one should "leave the door open one inch for miracles" (278)—while not plotting them —because, occasionally, if one has "confidence," prostitutes *do* turn out to be virgins.

The ideas represented by the Broadway "regulars" are epitomized in Movement, the novel's black and its most emphatic "missing person." According to Movement, the American Negro's real lack of any traditional or mythic roots makes him—in white eyes—the most "authentic" kind of American, for whom no foreign image has been imposed. Yet the White Americans, caged in by their own Puritan (Apollonian) heritage, have themselves imposed a certain identity on the blacks, one which reflects the whites' secret yearning to be free of restraint. The black man, they believe, because he is not "white," is *colorful*—and this quality connotes the exotic, the spicy, the forbidden.

"Authentic" black men, then, are those who have assumed the Dionysian pose expected of them: they smile, wear colorful clothing or ornaments, tell "folksy" tales of grandparents who were happy picking cotton, are "spontaneously" musical, and—hyperpotent (all attributes of the Negro admired by Mezz in *The Blues*). These characteristics, however, in the blacks who assume them are all confidence tricks designed to enhance the public relations of those blacks who wish to befriend the whites. Secretly, Movement notes, the black man has as great a wish to be orthodox as the white man has to be "colorful": "The authentic white American is often a would-be blackface minstrel man, and the authentic American Negro is often a Calvinist Negro impersonator" (152).

Movement, the Negro of the 1950's, is conceived as a black who is beginning to rebel against his "authentic" role, yet who cannot deny his own Calvinist (or Apollonian) yearnings—for Brooks Brothers suits, for correctly articulated speech, for white women. In his public relations with the white world, he learns at least to compromise between the "authenticity" white men demand and his own orthodox ideals: a single gold earring offsets "the curse" of his Madison Avenue suit; his sale of marihuana (the intoxicant of *The Blues*) is contrasted with his refusal to grin or to speak jive; his ability to play the bongo drums is coupled with his love of Beethoven; and his occasional efforts to perform sexual "magic" with such white girls as Betsy Bugbee (who are gratified only by the humiliation of being "attacked" by a "savage") are counteracted by his sadistic impulses and total impotence with black girls. Ironically, however, the novel's "cool" black is suffering from acute hypertension; internally, he is truly the "hot" black man that Betsy and Vanderbilt Bohlen want him to be.

The Risers, then, is a book which looks back both to *The Blues* and to *Limbo.* As in Wolfe's biography of Mezz, the Broadway novel concerns a social "frontier"—in this case Broadway, when some try to "cross the color line" and others seek a Dionysian extreme. Yet the influence of Wolfe's antiutopia is apparent as well: Mezz's myth is shattered by the "joke," by the masochistic tendency to provoke confidence tricks even in the "stories" of virgins. But independently of these highly "intellectual" ideas—which are likely to be overlooked in a parody of Damon Runyon—*The Risers* is probably one of Wolfe's *funniest* books: the puns, the practical jokes, the comic characterizations give the novel a lightness that Wolfe did not attempt again until *Come on Out, Daddy.*

III The Magic of Their Singing

Wolfe's third novel about a New York "fringe group" was published in 1961, two years before *The Risers* was to be reprinted as *Everything Happens at Night. The Magic of Their Singing* concerns three university students from Harvard and Bennington who, as "weekend beats," spend their leisure time with Greenwich Village blacks, homosexuals, and "hipsters"—a group unable by definition to reciprocate by visiting the white upper-middle-class centers of Connecticut.

The hero of the "beat" novel is Hoyt Fairliss, a graduate student in Harvard's Political Science Department who lost part of a leg in the Korean War, and one of whose ancestors had signed the Declaration of Independence. Typically for a Wolfean hero who is able to verbalize so many of the personal conflicts most people cannot acknowledge, his friends call him "the Examiner." In part, *The Magic* concerns Hoyt's "examination" of his own class and his inevitable rejection of the rather insincere life it offers for—again, typically—the "primitive island" (in this case the Middle East before the six-day war of 1967) where hard work and matrimony offer "healthier" rewards. But first, Hoyt has an opportunity to "examine" the alternatives: the kinds of lives his father ("Sam'l") would either call "dirty" or romanticize from a distance—that of the moneyless but "hip" groups of New York.

Hoyt's "slumming" companions during the night described in the novel are his girl friend, Penelope Gissings,[2] a student from Bennington given to Reichian excesses, and his roommate,

Worthington Rivers, who exemplifies everything objectionable about America's top classes: their extreme orthodoxy; their anti-Semitism; their "conspicuous consumption"—especially when someone with less money than themselves is near; their relative impotence with girls of their own class and their secret attraction to "dirty" black girls. Moreover, Worthington is as unscrupulous as he is unattractive. He not only attempts to "steal" Penelope from Hoyt, but he deserts his own date for the evening, a Shoshana Gasharid who has just arrived from Beirut to buy water pumps from Worthington's father. Shoshana's work in the Middle East, we learn, involves a number of confidence tricks put to good use. Her father was Colonel Boergensen, a Swedish diplomat of great honesty (in contrast to Sam'l) who had served on the United Nations Truce Commission in Palestine and was subsequently killed during a border incident.

Shoshana now reveals that her father's ancestors had been German Jews, a secret which the Israelis had discovered but which had not influenced the Colonel's scruples. In fact, he had founded the East Mediterranean Development Corporation, a nonprofit organization designed to ease the life of the Arabs, not by building the dams which make political headlines, but by contributing generators to small villages and fighting the disease called "bilharziasis." The Arabs, however, had refused to accept these gifts until they were made to believe that they were based on secrets stolen from the *Israelis*. Shoshana, the Swedish daughter of the Colonel (who was really Jewish), had subsequently been asked to *pose* as a Jewish counterspy and to "steal" Israeli technical material for the Arabs. At the time the novel begins, Shoshana is continuing the work of her father. In the United States, she reveals everything but her real Jewish origin to Worthington, who is supposed to help her buy supplies. Hoyt, of course, learns her complete story during their first meeting.

Eventually, Hoyt, Penelope, Worthington, and Shoshana meet in New York, first in a subway-station-turned-nightclub located under the Waldorf (a fashionable New York hotel). This club represents one of the haunts to which the supposedly liberal white man goes when he wishes to see "authentic" black musicians: those who incessantly grin, who play *real* New Orleans Jazz, who wear country-folksy clothes and blue suede shoes. (These, as we have noted, are characteristic of Wolfe's blacks as they are "invented" by white men.) The leader and spokesman for the jazz band is called History Jones, a black man who wears a Brooks Brothers suit when not performing and who secretly prefers "cool" jazz and "beat" talk to Dixieland and jive. In the same club the students also meet two professional "beats": Prosper Merrymake—"beat" poet, seller of "reefers," mambo instructor, possible schizophrenic; and Marga Countryman—black woman, dancer, shoplifter. Worthington is instantly attracted to Marga, the "dirty" black girl with whom all outrages are permissible; but at the same time, History finds in Penelope his dream of the ravishable *white* girl. The developing sexual tensions lead to a mass brawl, in which all visitors to the club participate.

Those who are able to leave the club before the arrival of the police gravitate to another club in the Village, a gathering place for "authentic beats," which is appropriately called "The End." There we are introduced to the novel's most interesting character, Lewellyn Period, a homosexual who specializes in "rough trade" (that is, a male prostitute who is hired specifically to perform sadistic-sexual acts). Lewellyn (who prefers to be called Lew-Ellen) is a rebel's rebel, who shuns both the "ordinary" and the "beat" orthodoxies and whose only credo is to do "everything" without being caught (arrested.) While the other characters become increasingly intoxicated after smoking reefers, Lewellyn tells Penelope that her sympathy for such "sensitive" criminals as Genet and Caryl Chessman is a form of discrimination against all less artistic "jailbirds."

The discussion continues in Prosper's apartment, where the black musicians, the students, the "beats," and Lewellyn immediately divest themselves of their clothing. Those who object—Hoyt and Shoshana—are bound and gagged before they can stop the fun. It then becomes clear that the "beats" in the novel must be divided into two categories: the impotent-initiators, like Lewellyn, and the remaining "sleepwalkers" whose needs are to be manipulated (cf. discussions of "pseudo-aggression" and "psychic-masochism" in preceding chapters). Taking advantage of the general intoxication, Lewellyn organizes the mass rape of Penelope by the black musicians. As a finality, Worthington is brought to Penelope's bed, but he is told that she is the Negress Marga, while Penelope is led to believe that she is again being attacked by History. Ironically, both experience their first real orgasm, which is precipitated by their mutually erroneous illusions of a black nightmare. Each had been associating sexual gratification with "fantasy violations"; and, while among the "beats," each had unconsciously sought the mythically supreme "violator": the black.

Eventually, Hoyt and Shoshana manage to rescue Penelope and call the police. After Penelope is hospitalized, Hoyt and Shoshana discuss the events of the evening and then plan to work in the Middle East together. Hoyt rationalizes his decision as follows: "The first reason for working hard during the day is to tire yourself out so that you will fall into bed at an early hour and so avoid nights like this one. The night becomes a tarantula to those who do no useful work during the day, who simply move compulsively to and fro" (229).

Significantly, the above passage could refer as easily to the events narrated in *The Risers,* which also take place in a single night, as in *The Magic*. Indeed, the similarities of the two "fringe" books are extensive. There are psychically related characters, as for instance, Betsy Bugbee and Penelope, Movement and History Jones, Frana and Shoshana, Don Kiefer and Hoyt Fairliss. There is an equal fascination with the influence of black culture on the American scene and with the occasional, often sexual, crossings of the color lines. Symbols in the two books resemble each other: the *mask* of the Broadway novel becomes the *disguise* in the "beat" novel, which is preoccupied with descriptions of, and conflicts about, clothing (in contrast, of course, to the nude sequence ending the narrative). And *The Magic* borrows certain themes which were predominant in *The Risers:* the interest in "missing persons" in the latter is close in conception to the numerous cases of "mistaken identity" in the former—Hoyt is often confused with Worthington (because they are both upper class), History with the kinds of blacks Mezz befriended in *The Blues,* Worthington with History and Penelope with Marga in the rape episode, and an Arab farmer with an Israeli soldier during the border incident in which Shoshana's father is killed.

Moreover, the "missing persons" of the Broadway novel are also related to the "displaced persons" of the beat novel. Shoshana in particular frequently compares the activities of *D.P.'s* on the borders of the Middle East with those on the psychic borders of New York. Fundamentally, the "beats" are viewed as the equals of the

Palestinian refugees in that both *really* wish to live in their respective homelands. If the "beats" chose alienation, voluntarily, it is because they are refused admission to America's top classes; their true yearning is to be *orthodox*, a yearning which is revealed by their *own* orthodoxy even as a "fringe" group (the relative standardization of their dress, their talk, their music). Like the Middle Eastern refugees, the "beats" act as a herd—even their sexual experiences occur en masse. Yet, while they huddle together, unlike the true rebel who is traditionally against all cult, the "beats" complain because "the fortress will not collapse merely through the magic of their presence" (225). In this way, they are similar to Rostov and the passive resistors in *The Great Prince Died* whose programs were ineffective and often self-defeating, in contrast to the Israelis described in *The Magic,* whose weapons and "blueprints for electrification" have achieved results.

If the "beats" wish to be orthodox, those who are orthodox have a secret wish to be "beat." In Penelope's case, however, the wish is father to the thought, although the "lady-hipster" never realizes that she "invents" the unorthodoxy of the "beats," as other members of her class "invent" the "authentic" Negro. Ironically, while Penelope searches for borders, her friends in Greenwich Village search for the homeland—and, after failing to find it, they seek retribution from the "lady" who crosses their path. Here, then, lies the supreme case of "mistaken identity": the "outward-bound and the inward-bound happen to find themselves in the same peripheral place at the same moment, [and] they both assume they're facing and heading the same way. It's not so. They're moving in opposite directions . . ." (228).

This mistaken identity, of course, is the master joke of the novel, a book as much devoted to the study of "jokes" as any of Wolfe's work. However, *The Magic* is especially preoccupied with the "Jewish joke." (Two or three such jokes are told during the narrative, and History speaks of the "Joosh" [josh] people.) Significantly, it is Worthington, the admitted anti-Semite, who tells the most offensive joke—to the black, History. But the point seems to be that the Worthingtons of the world are secretly as much attracted to the "dirty" Jews as to the "dirty" blacks, whom they imagine to be free of all Calvinist-Puritan restraints. While Penelope achieves orgasm by imagining the attacks of Jewish monsters, the novel's real Jewess—Shoshana—remains the most rational and nonmonstrous character in the book. Thus, we find that the images imposed upon "beats," blacks, and Jews by orthodox society are all very much alike: they represent a mirror image of America's Dionysian yearnings.

IV *The History of Movement*

By the standards of the 1970's, Wolfe's sociology seems to be only slightly less out of joint than *Really The Blues* must have seemed in the early 1960's. Clearly, in his fringe novels Wolfe tries to compensate the blacks for the literary racism of his first book. At the same time, he withdraws sympathy from characters like Mezz—who, in the final analysis, did little to help their black "friends" by encouraging white performers to take away the few good jobs available to black musicians in the 1940's. *Really the Blues* does, on the other hand, attempt to discuss, however misguidedly, the larger consequences of white oppression on black personalities and on the black people as a whole.

In *The Late Risers* and *The Magic of Their Singing,* Wolfe turns his attention exclusively to black personalities by choosing to characterize those blacks who not only wear Brooks Brothers suits, but who—typically for Wolfe—are able to articulate their problems in psychoanalytical terms. For Wolfe in the 1960's, racism is as much a symptom of ego failure among a handful of financially solvent or famous blacks as it is a set of conditions imposed upon the entire black community by white society. The "secret yearning for orthodoxy" is—and was—no doubt entirely alien to the blacks trying to survive on welfare money; "orthodoxy" may well be yet another image imposed on the black man from outside.

The one minority group Wolfe attacks openly and without apology is homosexuals, most notably Lewellyn in *The Magic.* Wolfe's homosexuals do not even have the redeeming psychic softenings of a Helder or Rostov. Their closest counterpart would be the conception of Stalin in *The Great Prince Died,* although even Wolfe's Stalin could be said to have possessed a certain astuteness and subtlety denied to *Lewellyn,* whose only "yearning" is for "beatings." Wolfe's unbending attitude toward homosexuality is compatible with Dr. Bergler's theories, who, in his book *Homosexuality: Disease or Way of Life?* (1956), unhesitatingly chooses "disease."

Finally, Wolfe's blanket condemnation of white fringe groups, especially the "beats" of the early 1960's, must be taken as one man's opinion of a people who have contributed much to American culture and counterculture, whatever the half-truth about *their* "secret orthodoxy." In *The Magic,* Wolfe's rather desperate attempt to characterize "hipster" pseudo-aggressiveness through the mythologically unconvincing device of a gang rape ultimately weakens the novel, which—as it stands—must be considered his least satisfying study of a contemporary "frontier."

CHAPTER 7

Come on Out, Daddy

I *Beyond the Fringe Novels*

AFTER the publication of *The Magic of Their Singing* in 1961 and the reprinting of *The Late Risers* under the title *Everything Happens at Night* in 1963, Wolfe's interest in New York nightlife appeared to have been satiated, and he looked, instead, westward to the Pacific, where Californian life styles amalgamize the extremes of American culture. There Wolfe wrote *Come on Out, Daddy* and *Move Up/Dress Up/Drink Up/Burn Up,* in which the black is replaced by the Mexican migrant worker; the Broadway prostitute, by the Hollywood starlet; the Greenwich Village "hipster," by the acid-head; the Harlem "frontier," by another in Tijuana.

Yet Wolfe's work of the mid-1960's does not abandon the hero whose "joke book" is taken seriously by the society he represents. In *Come on Out, Daddy,* Gordon Rengs writes self-parodying film scripts which are actually filmed by producers who cannot differentiate between art and artifice. Simon Dwire, the central figure of three short stories, ghost-writes sex manuals for a public as gullible as it is (Wolfe hints) psychically impotent. Unlike their predecessors, Martine and Rostov, however, the more recent heroes *deliberately* compromise their principles, writing their "bibles" on commission rather than as personal journals or as philosophical tracts. The easy corruption of Gordon and Simon occurs in a society where the "formula" is too well entrenched to need a political platform or a theoretical textbook; the "neurosis" which had struggled to gain official approval in Wolfe's early novels is now seen as an established part of American life.

II *Toward* Come on Out, Daddy

Gordon Rengs, the hero of Wolfe's Hollywood novel, is to some extent an autobiographical character. Like his creator, he is a New

York novelist who, after writing nine books that receive little critical or popular attention, works as a screenwriter for five years before leaving to write a novel about his experiences (obviously, *Come on Out, Daddy*). Wolfe's career as a screenwriter began in New York in 1955 with the writing of television plays for General Electric Theater, TV Playhouse, and the Armstrong Circle Theater. Eventually he moved to California, where he did the rewriting of an episode for a television serial entitled *The Troubleshooters*. The circumstances surrounding the job are used in "Agoraphobia and the Public Domain," a chapter in *Come on Out, Daddy*.

In the years 1959 to 1963, Wolfe held four jobs as a movie screenwriter, although none of the scripts he worked on at that time were ever actually filmed. In 1959, he worked on a script of "Peter and Catherine" (the prototype for the script Gordon Rengs is writing in the opening chapters of *Come on Out, Daddy*). In the following year, Wolfe wrote "The Playboy Story" for Tony Curtis, who was to have been cast in the role of Hugh Hefner. Moving to Twentieth Century Fox in 1963, Wolfe was asked by Darryl Zanuck, Jr., to adapt a novel called *Shock Treatment* for the screen, but the script was ultimately abandoned in favor of another written by a writer closer to the Hollywood "tradition." Around the same time, Henry Miller asked Wolfe to write a script of *Tropic of Cancer* for Embassy Productions, but this film version too was rejected in favor of one by another writer. As of this writing, however, Wolfe appears to have turned his back on screenwriting in order to devote himself to fiction.

No doubt because Wolfe has been a part of the Hollywood experience, his satire of the film industry in *Come on Out, Daddy* rings true. His view is that of an insider whose passionate knowledge of the studio system provides a sound basis for parody. In a publisher's blurb for the book, Henry Miller acknowledges Wolfe's special insight: "One feels that [Wolfe] knows his Hollywood inside out. More, that no living writer could add another word on the subject. . . . The hell of it is that so much of it is based on truth."

In terms of literary merit, Wolfe's book has been compared to Nathanael West's *The Day of the Locust,* Norman Mailer's *Deer Park*, and Budd Shulberg's *What Makes Sammy Run?*, all of which turn to the film industry as an appropriate symbol of

Gothic American decadence. In spite of its flaws, *Come on Out, Daddy* is notable as Wolfe's most mature study of "show business"—a subject which has continued to interest him since *Really the Blues'* preoccupation with Dixieland jazz.

III *The Plot*

Gordon, who comes to Hollywood to earn two thousand dollars a week, is an artist who "goes tangent"—like Bix Biederbecke in *Really the Blues* and Neen, *Limbo's* artist in the pay of the state. Ostensibly, Gordon decides to work on a movie about Charlemagne merely to support himself "between novels." But his incentive to leave the film world becomes increasingly fainter as his "chivalric" interests deepen. A casual liaison with Marion Huddlesfield, a food-fad and acid head, is superseded by an infatuation for Wilhelmena Sproulle, a black woman who wants to be a film star. Eventually, Gordon meets the ambitious Taffy Ames, whom he helps become a star before asking her to leave Hollywood and marry him. Meanwhile, in the course of his work for film and television studios, he has dealings with more than forty characters. Among the most memorable are Shelley Al Fresco, a homosexual producer; Farley Munters, character actor; Stan Wiss, agent; script writer Iwar Masso and his seventeen-year-old hopeful, Colby Jacks; Donnie Reach, a Mexican actor; Manolo Masferrer, a Spanish bullfighter and abortionist; Anthony Trilling, an "extra"; the prostitutes Marcianna and Cee-Cee Throngs; and film star Anson Luddie and his Mexican wife, a retired musical-comedy star, Essie Vellis.

The individual chapters of *Come on Out, Daddy,* some published as short stories in *Playboy* and in *Cavalier,* are self-contained. While Gordon is often, but not always, the central character, each chapter frequently involves different protagonists and settings. In the first, "The Girls Around Charlemagne," Gordon has arrived in Hollywood to write a script for Tony Curtis. He is initiated into the mores of California by "hipster" Marion Huddlesfield and into those of the film studio by Wilhelmena Sproulle, the black woman who believes that, because Gordon eats in the studio commissary, he has the power to make her a star. Gordon hesitatingly compromises himself, promising her the impossible—a part in a movie—in return for her favors, and thus he becomes a "true belonger" of Hollywood.

During Gordon's third month in Hollywood, the subject of the chapter "Marcianna and the Natural Carpaine in Papaya," he meets a third representative of the California woman, the prostitute Marcianna. Not until she realizes that Gordon is the author of her favorite novel (called *Messages, Hints*) does Marcianna reveal her true name—Mercy Brown—and her background. She is part Cherokee and had left her reservation with ambitions that were realized only through prostitution. When she meets Gordon, she is about to leave for New York, where she will work in a fancy brothel to support her daughter, Gloria, in a fashionable Beverly Hills home.

"Agoraphobia Is in the Public Domain" is written from the point of view of Gordon's agent, Jerry Willens. During a writers' strike in the film studios, Gordon attempts to write for television, although his plays about *agora*phobia—a fear of open spaces—are confused with *acro*phobia—a fear of heights. At the same time, he is involved briefly with Dorotheen Bowdon, a part-Osage television actress.

Farley Munters, a character actor from New York, recounts an incident involving Anthony Trilling, a grinning muscular "extra," and Norva Hameel, a Nordic ice skater and dancer, in "Anthony from Afar." Norva is one of the most spectacular and ambitious women on The Strip. Although she is known to date men over forty exclusively, Anthony imagines that she is infatuated with him. Nevertheless, Norva even refuses to come to the birthday party Anthony arranges for Farley, as do all the girls he invites; and he subsequently infuriates Gordon by taking out his anger on a dog. The next morning, Anthony's body is discovered in his apartment. A cryptic message reads "Too many of them too many," which Farley believes refers to all the "refusals" Anthony provoked before dying.

The narrative becomes more complex in "Tense in Tee-Jay," which is set in the Mexican fun city, Tijuana. Gordon is now forty-four, and he has been dating the blonde Taffy Ames, a model who was once the dark dancer, Norva Hameel. Taffy's agent, Stan Wiss, is programming her new "Image"—that of a Miss "all-American" "Daring-do." In Tijuana, Taffy free-falls from ten thousand feet into an arena where she fights a bull, with the help of matador and part-time abortionist Manolo Masferrer. In spite of the publicity she receives, Gordon is upset and revolted by runaway ambitions which threaten to mutilate Taffy's "meat." During their quarrel, she innocently smokes marihuana—thinking it an ordinary cigarette—and, while intoxicated, she admits having had an abortion in Tijuana after a "quick ten days in Acapulco" with actor Donnie Reach. Tortured by her latent Catholicism and by Gordon's anger, she begins to sense the value of life.

In "170 Apaches, if Possible," Gordon is at loose ends while Taffy is in Des Moines on a publicity tour. At present, he is working on the script of an "adult" Western and making notes for a new novel, but both projects are affected by depression and a writer's block. At the time, Hollywood is on the edge of panic because of Gary Cooper's death, and many members of the film industry—like sixty-year-old screenwriter Iwar Masso—hasten to health clubs where their own fleeting mortality might hopefully be allayed. In one of these clubs Iwar invites Gordon to a dinner party at the home of prostitute Cee-Cee Throngs and her husband, Benno. The couple, despite all their liberal sexual attitudes, are using Cee-Cee's earnings to invest in slum real estate, which they refuse to rent to blacks. Meanwhile, their small son, Jimsie, is being cared for by Iwar's teen-aged protégée, Colby Jacks, who wants to be a movie star. Half altruistically and half in the spirit of a practical joke, Gordon secretly arranges to have the girl sent back to her home in Pennsylvania before she becomes another Cee-Cee.

"The Going Price of Adoration" is the most involved and the richest chapter in the novel. Its action is set during the filming of Gordon's script of *The Roar of Charlemagne*. On the set, Gordon meets and befriends a movie idol, Anson Luddy, a "secret" intellectual who came to the film industry after an early disillusionment in the Spanish Civil War. The adventures of Anson related in the chapter are punctuated by the taut relationship of Gordon and Taffy, who quarrel about the conflict of marriage and career. Anson's problems, by contrast, concern his wife, Essie Vellis, the retired movie star, and his mistress, Dr. Joan Wexler, a child psychologist. Anson takes Gordon and Taffy to visit the retreat for the retarded where Joan works; and, after some pointed comparisons between actors and Mongoloids, the four drive to an aquarium. There, Anson is recognized by his fans and narrowly escapes being mangled by their "adoration." Subsequently, Joan leaves—

her move in the elaborate "game" that their relationship has become.

The remaining trio proceed to Big Sur, where Essie lives in seclusion, indulging in obsessive eating which has made her monstrously obese, a counterreaction to her husband's chronic nausea and weight loss. While the Luddys are involved in their caloric war, Taffy and Gordon slip away to a nearby bathhouse. Once inside, they discover that the bath is already occupied by producer Shelley Al Fresco and his homosexual friends. After Gordon manages to obtain a film of the party, he blackmails Shelley into hiring blacklisted actors, into starring Taffy in his next film, and into filming Gordon's novel-in-progress about Hollywood. Taffy's acceptance of stardom-through-blackmail, however, is not without its "price": inevitably, there is a deterioration of her relationship with Gordon.

The "price" is the central theme of "The Many Faces of Esperanza," which concerns the separation and eventual reconciliation of Gordon and Taffy. While Gordon flees to Yucatán, Taffy continues to pursue stardom. Now, however, she drinks before participating in the obligatory publicity gimmicks, and after one such stunt, Taffy, inebriated, runs through Hollywood in search of Gordon. Her directionless flight takes her to Wilshire Boulevard, which suddenly (and symbolically) caves in. Taffy's body is discovered by the excavators twenty feet down, next to several Indian artifacts. Gordon rejoins her in a convalescent home, where, for the first time, he, out of sympathy, accepts her uncritically. There he meets her parents—her Mexican mother and Swedish father (who has been Gordon's masseur)—and learns that Taffy's real name is Esperanza Effleurage Nordhoff. After her parents leave, Taffy and Gordon have their first successful sexual experience, after which Taffy announces that she is giving up acting because she is pregnant with Gordon's child. The couple then plan to leave Hollywood and marry.

The last chapter, "'Be Ye Ever Facetious and Abstemious,'" is written in the form of a *"First-draft screenplay with first-draft happyend"* (421). It is essentially a Surreal montage, set out like a shooting script, of many of the characters and circumstances used in the preceding chapters. Insofar as it has a plot, the script concerns a farewell dinner Gordon gives for his acquaintances on

Academy Award night. While the guests watch the awards on television, Gordon announces his intention of raising his child on Lakrabos, "a very small island in the Aegean where there isn't one movie house" (426).

IV *The Form*

Despite the episodic quality of *Come on Out, Daddy,* which is structured like a collection of short stories, there is a thematic development that allows the book to be treated as a loosely integrated novel. This development, however, is confined to the personalities of Gordon and Taffy, both of whom represent the dilemma of the artist self-corrupted. Gordon, in this context, is the traditional male artificer of, in his case, novels, while Taffy is an artist simply because, in Wolfe's view, she is a woman. For Wolfe (who had been attacking the concept of Mother the Monster in every preceding book), the biological ability of women to "create" children is a superartistic endeavor, requiring, in the age of contraceptives, an inspiration and a commitment equal to that of the conventional male "artist."

The film industry offers an opportunity to study the corruption of both types of artists, male and female, because it is set apart from the everyday world in which writers write novels and women have babies. In essence, the artist is actively prevented from practicing his art in Hollywood and then rewarded for his inactivity, as is Gordon when he is paid two thousand dollars for changing seven words in a script. It is suggested that the *real* artist comes to Hollywood ostensibly for money but actually to avoid creation. Similarly, women come to the film industry to become movie stars, but also perhaps to avoid motherhood. (Hence the interest in abortion in the novel.) Significantly, Gordon and Taffy must avoid the industry to produce. Gordon writes novels in the interim between scriptwriting jobs, and Taffy will bear a child (after the close of the novel) when she has given up her Hollywood ambitions.

Structurally, then, *Come on Out, Daddy* concerns the artist in conflict with society (as it is represented by the film industry). In Gordon's case, by the third chapter he has gone beyond the restrictions of movie scriptwriting to even more formulated work on television scripts. Immediately after, he leaves Hollywood briefly to write a novel, and then, in the fourth chapter, he meets Norva-Taffy. The two events are a turning point, after which the Hollywood temptations of success and sexual freedom become increasingly ungratifying. In the concluding chapters, Gordon slowly becomes estranged from the Hollywood environment, by refusing to play the required social "games" and by indulging in a number of practical "jokes" at the expense of the industry—returning Colby to her parents, blackmailing Shelley, writing surreal-satirical screenplays. Eventually, he leaves Hollywood resolved to be a full-time novelist. The development of Taffy, by contrast, moves through a progressively self-limiting escape from Wolfe's view of femininity, involving instead promiscuous relations with film executives, an abortion, dangerous publicity stunts, and "humiliating" the man she loves (Gordon) by forcing him to take his blackmail "joke" seriously before her final acceptance of motherhood.

The remaining characters represent Gordon and Taffy "trapped" in various phases of the typical Hollywood career. The circumstances surrounding the women, in particular, frequently parallel those of Taffy at some point in her life (or they demonstrate the possibilities open to her if she were to remain an actress). Marcianna and her sixteen-year-old daughter, who can go to Beverly Hills High School with the "rich kids" because her mother prostitutes herself to earn a Hollywood income, have affinities with Taffy and her parents, who disown their daughter in the interests of her career. Colby, at seventeen, begins her Hollywood career under the "tutelage" of the elderly Iwar Masso, as did Taffy under the similar "tutelage" of Farley Munters, Donnie Reach, and Gordon. By twenty-two, Wilhelmena Sproulle knows that all the auditions are held in bed. Cee-Cee Throngs, approaching thirty, no longer prostitutes herself for stardom but simply for money. And the middle-aged Essie Vellis (Taffy-Esperanza's namesake), at two hundred and fifty pounds, survives as the physical counterpart of all that is psychically monstrous in the Hollywood woman.

Similarly, reflections of Gordon (and the relatively intact Farley Munters, who regards acting as just another nine-to-five job) are found in Anthony's paranoia, in Donnie Reach's search for potency, in Iwar Masso's terror of death, and most spectacularly in Manolo Masferrer, who will kill bulls or embryos with equal fervor. Like Manolo, Gordon participates in a death game by "killing" his art, his self-respect, his chance for happiness with a woman.

If Gordon and Taffy are able to avoid the fate of their colleagues, it is because (characteristically) they are both engaged in self-therapy throughout the course of the novel. Taffy's desperate run and the collapse of Wilshire Boulevard, toward the end of the novel, represent the final shattering of her "basic fallacy" (Bergler) about stardom. Her "cure" had begun in early chapters with a small number of compromises she had been able to make with her "neurosis": her acknowledgment of death in Tijuana; her shock of recognition at the sight of Essie Vellis; her acceptance of Gordon's separate will; and, in "The Many Faces of Esperanza," the blow to her sense of omnipotence gained through her loss of coordination while inebriated and through the pain experienced during and after the cave-in. Her (and Gordon's) ultimate "health" is achieved by leaving a "sick" society for an island which has remained unaffected by the mechanized world.

V *Psychic Infancy*

According to Gordon, Hollywood's preoccupation with fantasy is "unhealthy" because it bleeds into real life. The movie about Charlemagne, for instance, is less about the historical figure than about Tony Curtis. And the star who even momentarily steps out of his role as star—as Anson Luddy does by criticizing a southern fan's politics—risks being mobbed. In short, Hollywood is a place where media, message, and maker are indistinguishable: people constantly act as if in front of a camera, and the world's trivia is there forced to be "larger than life."

The direct consequence (or cause) of this characteristic is suggested by the most pervasive image found in *Come on Out, Daddy*—that of the infant. The star system and the infantile fantasy are frequently associated in the novel because, it seems, those who choose not to have babies are psychic infants themselves. Anthony Trilling, for example, is a secret thumb-sucker. Marion Huddlesfield endorses fruitarians who are "sweet smelling, like babies" (27). California is called "one big play pen" (290); the spa at Big Sur is an "embryonic dunk" (341); and a dented fender looks like "a baby's plump bottom" (373). These allusions to infancy refer to a desperate and impossible clinging to the "megalomania" (Bergler) which is normally—we learned in *Limbo*—discarded in early childhood. In Hollywood and the society it typifies, reality is rejected to keep megalomania (the sense of immortality and self-sufficiency) intact.

A study of the individual chapters of the Hollywood novel, from this point of view, becomes a catalogue of Berglerian symptoms of neurosis: the regression to infancy, the consequences of regression (anxiety and "psychic masochism"), and the defense against the consequences ("pseudo-aggression"). In the remaining space, it is perhaps worth mentioning a few of the devices Wolfe uses to convey this complex psychoanalytic thesis.

Beyond the images of infancy, the descriptions of Joan Wexler's retarded patients, and the continual references to Indians (suggesting the infancy of America), one of the most notable indications of neurosis is what Gordon calls the "packaging mentality" of the film world. "Packaging" as a kind of rationalization associated with the infant before he can differentiate between "self" and "other" has been treated before in *Limbo*'s "consistency" and in *The Great Prince Died*'s "centralism." In *Come on Out, Daddy*, the same idea is expressed by film-studio terminology: the "package deal" was at one time an in-studio contract covering a *team* of actors and technicians. By the time Gordon reaches Hollywood in the 1950's, the "package deal" has proliferated to larger areas of life. Now, the studios not only make films but "provide the necessary transportation and, further, living quarters for the viewers" (218) through investments in real estate and road works. Hollywood's involvement in nonfilmic enterprises indicates—to Gordon—its grandiose idea of itself as the core of the world. The Hollywood executive, captivated by this delusion, shares the idea with the Stalinists in *The Great Prince* that the public is a "grey mass" whose passions are predictable and manipulatable, the same idea that the infant has of the people who take care of it. Periodically, however, the "grey mass" resists "packaging" through "spasms" in which, in the name of "adoration," they tear such stars as Anson Luddy to bits.

Additional evidence of megalomania is found in the practice of changing one's "image" or "presence" in Hollywood. Fundamentally, this characteristic is related to the infantile idea of self-determination, to the belief that the infant is his own creation, which is transformed into the film industry's belief that it can "create" a star. Through the narrative material involving Taffy's career in particular, we witness a process of reconstruction which involves frequent changes of name, appearance, and style, until the original "self" of the actor has been completely absorbed into the "system." In essence, the practice of "cutting off" the natural attributes of the actor and of replacing them with more streamlined ones is similar to *Limbo*'s "voluntary amputation" and *The Great Prince*'s annihilation of undesirable elements in the Communist party.

In Hollywood, however, "Image" changing is all the more perpetual because it is grounded on the aura of youth. Ill health, wrinkles, excess poundage, and gray hair are an anathema in the film world, whose existence depends upon the fiction that its stars never age (or grow up). Gordon remarks that the actor who gives any indication of maturity "is a traitor to the perennial two-year-old inside his fan, and is to be torn limb from limb for succumbing to the clock and the calendar it was his whole function to negate" (272). Thus, even an established actor is obsessively concerned about his body's minutiae, an indication, for Wolfe, of a secret conviction that it is as easy to control existence as it is to control hair color.

The "psychic infants" of Hollywood, moreover, are basically adults who have been trapped in the "oral phase" (the time in infancy when the mouth was the most sensitized part of the body) and who still believe that the "septet of baby fears" (Bergler) are viable. The fears are indicated by the high susceptibility of various characters to phobia, as in Marion Huddlesfield's hypochondria, Gordon's claustrophobia, Dorotheen Bowdon's agoraphobia, Taffy's acrophobia, and the collective phobias of the entire television industry outlined in the chapter called "Agoraphobia Is in the Public Domain."

The "oral" inclinations of the film industry, by contrast, are suggested by what might be called "symbolic cannibalism." Human relationships in Hollywood, observes Anson's valet, Luis, follow the laws of the science of ecology, wherein "in any community of living things, all eat on all, in a most delicate nutritional balance" (353). Anson Luddy and his wife, Essie, through their obsessive starvation and eating, validate Luis' comment and draw parallels with the obliquely cannibalistic relationship of Gordon and Taffy. But, beyond the narrative material dealing directly with ingestion,

Wolfe uses such stock phrases as "The world is making a meal of me" and "You're eating me alive" (frequently repeated at the climax of individual chapters), as well as the novel's settings (coffeehouses, vegetarian restaurants, film-set lunch wagons, cocktail lounges, dinner parties, the studio commissary, a strip show in which spectators literally "taste" the girls) to indicate the force of "oral" or ecological interests. Hovering in the background, it might be added, are the ferocious appetites of the fans for the insatiably hungry stars.

VI *What to Do About Hollywood*

Characteristically for Wolfe, the problem of "psychic infancy" is related to the theory of happiness put forth in Freud's *Civilization and Its Discontents.* If Joan Wexler's Mongoloid patients are "happy," it is because their infantile delusions are incapable of being challenged, because they do not have the mental equipment to perceive reality. Furthermore, in the retreat they are insulated from the society that ordinarily demands that its individuals forfeit at least the rudiments of megalomania by learning to feed and care for themselves. But the retarded are fortunate (as are the Anti-Pros in *Limbo*) in that society is prepared to make special concessions for at least those whose parents are wealthy.

For the remaining characters in the novel, whose "infancy" is psychic, not genetic, there is a constant struggle between reality and dream which is antithetical to "happiness." Instead of providing retreats, society (and the laws of nature) presents insurmountable obstacles to the realization of total megalomania. In their discovery that there is no way back to the crib, the citizens of Hollywood are faced with the collapse of their "fun culture" (290) that is symbolized by the collapse of Wilshire Boulevard. Instead of "happiness," the members of the film colony are left at the mercy of their acute anxiety, which leads to the evils of the star system.

The solution that Gordon discovers is markedly similar to Martine's in *Limbo* and to Paul's in *The Great Prince.* Fundamentally, one must relinquish megalomania and thereby free the creative aspects of personality. Men must cease "going tangent," even if it means the loss of two thousand dollars a week, and concern themselves with a "reasonably reality-grounded and more or less adultized project" (237); and women must acknowledge, in the novel's most debatable conclusion, that "traditionally men *are* selfish punks. Some women have managed to live with that fact, and even extract a bit of pleasure from it" (336). In short, Wolfe—the disillusioned Trotskyite—suggests that the kind of life ordinarily greeted with a degree of contempt as "bourgeois" might be the nearest approach to "happiness" in contemporary society.

CHAPTER 8

What to Do About Bernard Wolfe

IN a sense, all of Wolfe's fiction can be taken as a repudiation of his experiences up until the very late 1940's, when he became acquainted with the theories of Dr. Bergler and, simultaneously, began his work on *Limbo.* His political experiences with Trotsky, his reaction to the civil war in Spain, his association with Greenwich Village bohemians, his contribution to popular-science magazines, his ghost-written gossip column, his quest for the "authentic Negro"—together, these represent the sum total of an early radical and "fringe-group" life style Wolfe obsessively reconsiders and rejects in novel after novel. Wolfe's writing seems to be a personal act of intellectual exorcism, even when he ostensibly deals with contemporary ideologies and institutions—so haunting does the mythology of his youth appear to be.

Yet, it is precisely the complex psychoanalytic vision Wolfe attempts through the act of exorcism that ultimately justifies a body of work seemingly committed to purely topical interests and "relevant" issues. This vision is what is unique in Wolfe's fiction. Perhaps no other novelist has risked so explicit a neo-Freudian study of society. In Wolfe's fiction, characters are created as mouthpieces for Dr. Bergler's special school of psychoanalysis: Bergler's terminology is used; symptoms are described; plot developments have parallels with Bergler's course of treatment. Wolfe's most urgent theme deals with Bergler's "one neurosis"—"psychic masochism"—and its effects on the more spectacular and—for Wolfe—ominous characteristics of modern history.

Politically, Wolfe uses Dr. Bergler's theories to remove himself from the arena. He sees no solution to the problem of fascism because, in his view, the political man (even in the opposition) is motivated by "pseudo-aggression" and is thus morally unacceptable as a liberator. The healthy man, on the other hand, is pretty much apolitical by definition; he discovers "jokes" in the literal readings of all ideologies, and, throwing up his hands at the whole messy business, he retreats to a primitive island (of one sort or another) where the distinction between "healthy aggression" and "pseudo-aggression" is less likely to be obscured. Meanwhile, Wolfe suggests, oppressed and Third World people have cultural values and resources entirely alien to those of (any) government, which permit them to survive despite interference from above.

If Wolfe's politics as embodied by virtually all of the heroes of his novels is somehow appropriate for a disillusioned Trotskyite who lived through the traumatic 1930's and 1940's, they hardly appeal to the apocalyptic 1960's and 1970's. Even more idiosyncratic for some of his readers is Wolfe's attitude toward women. Although privately Wolfe claims he has "always" been in favor of Women's Liberation, he follows Bergler's suggestion that women are psychologically "gifted" beings who are able to find healthy masochistic pleasure *only* in a total surrender to the natural sexual aggressiveness of men. Many of Wolfe's heroines eventually give up their ambitions to become housewives, after experiencing what is for Wolfe the *only* valid sexual pleasure a woman can achieve: a vaginal orgasm, with the man in the top-most position. Both Bergler and Wolfe insist that only 10 percent of American women are healthy enough even to attempt this very special form of gratification.

It may be a final irony that Wolfe was never able to see the "joke" in Dr. Bergler's books. However, the peculiar dilemma for the readers of Wolfe is that we can attack him for his psychology and his politics, while, at the same time, we can admire his courage as a spokesman for such wildly unorthodox views and find lasting value in their expression in the esthetics of his marvelously complex and playful novels. Wolfe must inevitably find a place in the history of modern American literature as a master of satire and parody as well as a literary propagandist for his own maddeningly consistent and flagrantly outrageous ideas. He must also be remembered as one of our best raconteurs, a contemporary Damon Runyon with the sophisticated vision of a Huxley or an Orwell.

Bernard Wolfe is not at the end of his career. Three new novels are in various stages of completion as of this writing: one, to be called "The Picker," promises to be a new masterwork of more than a thousand pages. Meanwhile, on the basis of *Limbo* and *The Great Prince Died* alone, Wolfe remains too interesting and vital a writer for him to retire to those primitive islands that have beckoned so seductively in the last pages of his books.

Notes and References

Chapter Two

1. Friedrich Nietzsche, *The Birth of Tragedy in the Spirit of Music* in *The Birth of Tragedy and the Genealogy of Morals,* trans. Francis Golffing (Garden City, New York, 1956), p. 43.

2. *Ibid.*, p. 23.

Chapter Three

1. Martine's theory about the twin instincts was inspired by Freud's *Beyond the Pleasure Principle.*

2. Bergler returned the compliment by mentioning *Limbo* in *Laughter and the Sense of Humor* (New York, 1956), p. 287, in reference to the connection between masochism and laughter. According to the analyst, the Amps are humorless because, with masochism officially approved, "even the ego must be satisfied. Thus it is no longer necessary to deflate the superego's accusation by means of laughter."

3. The most detailed discussion of "psychic masochism" can be found in Bergler's *The Battle of Conscience* (Washington, D.C., 1948) and *The Basic Neurosis* (New York, 1949).

4. Bergler rejects Freud's view of the Oedipal mother as the cause of neurosis, accepting instead Freud's late suggestion that the pre-Oedipal mother is more important for the developing personality. The "basic neurosis," according to Bergler, originates in the "oral phase" —the first year or so of childhood.

5. The word is borrowed from Georg Groddeck's *The Book Of the It* (New York, 1961).

6. Bergler describes a three-layered structure for all such neurotic symptoms, composed of an unconscious wish, an inhibition of the wish, and a defense against the inhibition.

7. According to statements in Bergler's *Neurotic Counterfeit-Sex* (New York, 1951), men can experience an orgasm which is *not* pleasurable. (Cf. Martine's sexual experiences with Ooda in Part I of *Limbo.*)

8. There are also historical and literary associations for many names. Ubu is taken from Alfred Jarry's surrealistic play *Ubu Roi,* Martine

from Martin Luther (another author of a "joke book?"), Vishinu from Vychinsky (the state prosecutor at the Moscow Trials), Rambo from Rimbaud, and Brother Theo from the brother of Van Gogh.

Chapter Five

1. *The Militant*, III (April 28, 1934).

2. The character of Sheridan Justice was inspired by that of Oliver Law, a black Brigadier who actually died in a similar way. Wolfe claims he obtained his information from novelist William Herrick, who wrote his version of the incident in *¡Hermanos!* (New York, 1969).

Chapter Six

1. Significant in this context is the surname of Benny O. Bliss, a name Wolfe used again for the byline of pseudonymously published articles.

2. The name of this character informs us that, in part, the novel is intended to parody Homer's *Odyssey*. In Wolfe's version, it is the *wife* (or girl friend) who travels to distant lands (Greenwich Village) and who is subsequently raped by her suitors. Penelope's last name, Gissings, suggests George Gissing, a late nineteenth-century novelist who wrote about lowlife in London.

Selected Bibliography

PRIMARY SOURCES

1. Books by Bernard Wolfe (listed chronologically)

How to Get a Job in the Aircraft Industry. By Berne [*sic*] Wolfe. Ed. by John M. Caldwell. Research by Neil F. Harrison. Mount Vernon, New York: Wallach Publications, 1943. [Softbound.]

Really the Blues. By Mezz Mezzrow and Bernard Wolfe. New York: Random House, 1946.

Limbo. New York: Random House, 1952.

The Late Risers: Their Masquerade. New York: Random House, 1954.

In Deep. New York: Knopf, 1957.

The Great Prince Died. New York: Scribner's, 1959.

The Magic of Their Singing. New York: Scribner's, 1961.

Come on Out, Daddy. New York: Scribner's, 1963.

Reading for Men: Come on Out, Daddy by Bernard Wolfe; *Death and Circumstance* by Hilary Waugh. Garden City, New York: Doubleday [n.d.]. Scribner's 1963 edition of *Come on Out, Daddy* issued in the same binding as Waugh's novel.

Everything Happens at Night. New York: New American Library, 1963. A reprint of *The Late Risers* in paperback.

Move Up/ Dress Up/ Drink Up/ Burn Up. Garden City, New York: Doubleday, 1968.

2. Books Ghost-Written for Bernard Wolfe by Raymond Rosenthal

Plastics, What Everyone Should Know. Indianapolis: The Bobbs-Merrill Company, 1945.

Hypnotism Comes of Age: Its Progress from Mesmer to Psychoanalysis. By Bernard Wolfe and Raymond Rosenthal. Indianapolis: The Bobbs-Merrill Company, 1948.

3. Translation

Hostovský, Egon. *The Plot.* Trans. by Alice Baker with Bernard Wolfe. Garden City, New York: Doubleday, 1961.

4. Separately Published Chapters of Novels by Bernard Wolfe

"La Rage de Vivre," *Les Temps Modernes,* No. 56 (June, 1950). First chapter of *Really The Blues.* [Trans. by Madeleine Gautier and Marcel Duhamel.]

"The Private Life of a Press Agent," *American Mercury,* LXXIII (December, 1951). Excerpt from *The Late Risers* with changes and glossary.

"Looking for Minnie," *American Mercury,* LXXIV (May, 1952). Excerpt from *The Late Risers.*

"The Man with the Rubber Nose, or One Soluble Spoon After Another," *American Mercury,* LXXV (December, 1952). Excerpt from *The Late Risers.*

"Happy Standing Up," *Nugget,* I (October, 1956). A condensation of several episodes taken from *The Late Risers.*

"Bus from Derby," *The Dude,* II (September, 1957). First chapter of *The Magic of Their Singing.*

"Miss Shoshana," *Dial,* I (March, 1960). Chapter 9 of *The Magic of Their Singing.*

"Really the Blues," *The Drug Experience.* Ed. by David Ebin. New York: Orion Press, 1961. Two excerpts from *Really the Blues.*

"Come on Out, Daddy," *Playboy,* VIII (February, 1961). Part I of *Come on Out, Daddy.*

"Marcianna and the Natural Carpaine in Papaya," *Playboy,* VIII (June, 1961). Reprinted in *The Bedside Playboy.* Ed. by Hugh M. Hefner. Chicago: Playboy Press, 1963. Part II of *Come on Out, Daddy.*

"Agoraphobia Is in the Public Domain," *Playboy,* VIII (November, 1961). Part III of *Come on Out, Daddy* with changes.

"Anthony from Afar," *Playboy,* IX (February, 1962). Reprinted in *The Twelfth Anniversary Playboy Reader.* Ed. by Hugh M. Hefner. Chicago: Playboy Press, 1965. Part IV of *Come on Out, Daddy* with changes.

"170 Apaches, if Possible. Part I." By Andrew Foxe [pseud. of Bernard Wolfe], *Cavalier* (August, 1963). From Part VI of *Come on Out, Daddy.*

"170 Apaches, if Possible. Part II." By Andrew Foxe [pseud. of

Bernard Wolfe], *Cavalier* (September, 1963). From Part VI of *Come on Out, Daddy.*

"The Going Price for Adoration," *Playboy,* X (October, 1963). From Part VII of *Come on Out, Daddy* with changes.

5. Popularized Scientific and Maritime Articles

"Saving a Ship for Uncle Sam," *Popular Science Monthly,* CXLII (February, 1943). Concerns the attempt to salvage the French line Normandie from New York's North River.

"Cheating the Axis Torpedoes," *Popular Science Monthly,* CXLII (March, 1943). An imaginary merchant mariner named Marty (a predecessor of Martine?) is saved by a rubber life suit when his ship is torpedoed.

"Getting the Convoys Through," *Popular Science Monthly,* CXLII (May, 1943). Concerns the merchant marines stationed on cargo ships bound for enemy waters.

"Putting More Speed and Power into Our New Navy," *Popular Science Monthly,* CXLII (June, 1943). Concerns the navy's research plant in Carderock, Maryland.

"These Are The Badges of Courage." By Bernard Wolf [*sic*], *Popular Science Monthly,* CXLIII (July, 1943). Concerns medals awarded to members of the armed forces during World War II.

"American Da Vinci," *Mechanix Illustrated,* XXXI (December, 1943). Concerns "one of America's greatest original scientists," Dr. George Speri Sperti.

"Streamlined Science Machine," *Mechanix Illustrated,* XXXI (January, 1944). Part II of article on Dr. Sperti.

"Model T of Helicopters," *Mechanix Illustrated,* XXXI (February, 1944). Concerns the PV-2 helicopter.

6. Miscellaneous Uncollected Pieces

"Floating Fashions." By Raymond Rosenthal and Bernard Wolfe, *Cosmopolitan,* CXXII (March, 1947). Concerns Armand Winfield, Greenwich Village designer of plastic jewelry.

"Uncle Remus and The Malevolent Rabbit," *Commentary,* VIII (July, 1949). Reprinted as "L'oncle Rémus et son Lapin," trans. by René Guyonnet, *Les Temps Modernes* (May, 1959). Exposes black aggression in Uncle Remus tales.

"Ecstatic in Blackface," *Modern Review,* III (January, 1950). Reprinted as "Ecstase en Noir," *Les Temps Modernes* (September, 1950) [no trans.]. Reprinted again *The Scene Before You:*

A New Approach to American Culture. Ed. by Chandler Brossard. New York: Rinehart, 1955. Discusses stereotype of "authentic Negro."

"War Bonds: More Delusions of Security." By Christopher Bliss [pseud. for Bernard Wolfe], *American Mercury*, LXXII (April, 1951). An attack on misleading advertising used to sell war bonds.

"José Schenck, Reverse the Charges" (short story), *American Mercury*, LXXXIII (July, 1951). "Con Man" in Mexico fantasizes about Hollywood producer.

"Self-Portrait" (short story), *Galaxy Science Fiction Magazine* (November, 1951). Reprinted in *The Robot and the Man*. Ed. by Martin Greenberg. New York: Gnome Press, 1953. An abbreviated *Limbo*.

"Are Taxes Making Liars of Us All?" by Christopher Bliss [pseud. for Bernard Wolfe], *American Mercury*, LXXIV (March, 1952). Humorous article on tax evasion.

"The Dot and the Dash Bird" (short story), *Playboy*, XI (December, 1954). Television scriptwriter deals with malevolencies of both his mother-in-law and a myna bird.

"Angry at What?" *Nation*, CLXXXVII (November 1, 1958). A critical look at four "beat" novels.

"Christmas in Balikpapan" (playlet), *Nugget*, II (February, 1959). O Henry-type tale of Christmas in Hollywood.

"The Man Who Murdered Trotsky," *Coronet*, XLVI (July, 1959). An account of the historical material treated in *The Great Prince Died*.

"The 'Darks' Against the 'Lights,'" *Esquire*, LIII (April, 1960). First published as a pamphlet kept in the humidors of the Twenty-one Club in New York City. An essay on the delights of cigar smoking.

"Manners and Morals on the Sunset Strip," *Esquire*, LVI (August, 1961). Description of Hollywood as a "company town."

"Swimming in Red Ink," *Playboy*, XI (July, 1964). Reprinted in *The Playboy Book of Humor and Satire*. Selected by the editors of *Playboy*. Chicago: Playboy Press, 1967. Humorous account of swimming pool constructed on Wolfe's property.

"Playboy Interview: Henry Miller," *Playboy*, XI (September, 1964).

"Sue Me Rich" (short story), *Playboy*, XI (October, 1964). Alternate ending for *Come on Out, Daddy*.

"A Pair of Jokers and an Ace," *Book Week* in *The Sunday Herald Tribune* (July 25, 1965). A review of Jack Warner's *My First Hundred Years in Hollywood*, Ronald Reagan's *Where's the*

Rest of Me?, and Josef Von Sternberg's *Fun in a Chinese Laundry*.

"The Man Called I-l-l-y-a," *The New York Sunday Times Magazine* (October 24, 1965). Article about David McCallum, the television actor who plays Illya Kuryakin in *The Man From U.N.C.L.E.* series.

"How Simon Got His Bureau" (short story), *Playboy*, XIII (February, 1966). First Simon Dwire story, set in Greenwich Village, satirizes "hipster" sexuality.

"The Step After Muscle," *Cosmopolitan*, CLX (February, 1966). A historical glance at changes in sexual stereotypes.

"The Roach Powder in the Maple Walnut" (short story), *Playboy*, XIII (May, 1966). Second Simon Dwire story satirizes Eric Berne's transactional analysis.

"Thirty Years After Stalin's Great Purge," *The New York Sunday Times Magazine* (September 18, 1966). An account of the Moscow Trials, similar to material used in *The Great Prince Died*.

"The Trouble with Harry," *Book Week* in the *World Journal Tribune* (March 26, 1967). Review of Bob Thomas' biography of Hollywood executive Harry Cohn, *King Cohn*.

"The 10 Percenters of Hollywood," *The New York Times Magazine* (June 18, 1967). Concerns talent agents in Hollywood.

7. Stories collected in *Move Up/ Dress Up/ Drink Up/ Burn Up*

"How Simon Did Not Become a Tree Surgeon." Simon Dwire smuggles "hot" television sets into Mexico, then encounters marihuana cultists.

"Constanta's Upset Stomach." Mexico heroine spies on secret right-wing militia men in training.

"Mr. Economos and the Sand Painters." Same setting and characters as in *Come on Out, Daddy*. Indian woman "persecutes" white actor.

"All Thumbs." Excerpt from *The Late Risers*.

"One I Forgot." Originally published as "The Hot Sauces of Magda" in *Playboy*, XV (February, 1968). Humorous tale about Mexican braceros.

"The Grave of His Case." Story of narcissistic actor inspired by Anson Luddy of *Come on Out, Daddy*.

"Chooky at War." Berglerian-type case history of compulsive gambler.

"Anything You Say." Set in Hollywood steakhouse.

"The Never-Ending Penny." Originally published in *Playboy*, VII

(September, 1960). Reprinted in *The Playboy Book of Science Fiction and Fantasy.* Selected by the editors of *Playboy.* Chicago: Playboy Press, 1966. Fable about Diosdado, peon of *The Great Prince Died.*

8. The Column in *Nugget*

"Wolfe's Den," *Nugget,* II (May, 1957). Concerns Elvis Presley, Tennessee Williams, Mckenna-Marshall recording of *Ulysses.*

"The Once Over," *Nugget,* II (June, 1957). Concerns filming of *Twelve Angry Men,* Frank Sinatra, Brian Keith, Sid Caesar.

"The Once Over," *Nugget,* II (July, 1957). Sid Caesar, Susan Strasberg in *Stage Struck,* Arnold Shulman's *A Hole in the Head.*

"Once Over," *Nugget,* II (August, 1957). "Bop" and Nietzsche, Walter Gellhorn's *Individual Freedom and Governmental Restraints,* bureaucratic pressures on television.

"Once Over," *Nugget,* II (September, 1957). O'Neill's *Long Day's Journey into Night* and the nature of tragedy, Peter De Vries' *The Tunnel of Love,* Rosenberg and Manning's *Mass Culture: The Popular Arts In America,* Tennessee Williams' treatment of the Negro.

"Once Over," *Nugget,* III (October, 1957). Satiric view of television, Marilyn Monroe, Nathanael West, miscegenation in *Island in the Sun.*

"Once Over," *Nugget,* II (November, 1957). Jazz and class consciousness, film epics, Robert Peel Smith's *"Where Did You Go?" "Out" "What Did You Do?" "Nothing."*

"Once Over," *Nugget,* III (February, 1958). Nabakov's *Lolita,* Cozzens' *By Love Possessed,* Kerouac's *On the Road.*

9. Television Scripts

Assassin! Produced by TV Playhouse on February 20, 1955, at 9:00 P.M. (EST) on Channel 4 in New York. One-hour play about Trotsky's death and the trial of his assassin. Wolfe later turned the play into the novel, *The Great Prince Died.*

The Ghost Writer. Produced by TV Playhouse on May 29, 1955, at 9:30 P.M. (EST) on Channel 4 in New York. A former actor discovers, while running for Congress, that the daughter of his rival is working for him.

"The Five Who Shook the Mighty." Produced by Circle Theatre on March 20, 1956 at 9:30 P.M. (EST) on Channel 4 in New

York. The trial of five Romanians who had captured the Romanian Communist Legation in Switzerland.

SECONDARY SOURCES

1. Articles and Sections of Books

GALLOWAY, DAVID. "An Erratic Geography: The Novels of Bernard Wolfe," *Critique: Studies in Modern Fiction,* VII (Spring, 1964). Perceptive description of all the novels; favors *The Magic of Their Singing* and *Come on Out, Daddy.*

KAZIN, ALFRED. "The Ghost of Leon Trotsky." *Contemporaries.* Boston: Little, Brown and Company, 1962. Attack on the psychoanalytical bent of *The Great Prince Died.*

2. Reviews

BOROFF, DAVID. "The Beat in Counterpoint," *The Saturday Review of Literature,* XLIV (July 8, 1961). Favorable review of *The Magic of Their Singing* and recognition of Wolfe's talent.

GOLD, HERBERT. "The Pride and the Guilt," *The Nation,* CLXXXIII (April 4, 1959). Favorable review of *The Great Prince Died* and recognition of Wolfe as a "serious" novelist.

KNIGHT, ARTHUR. "Movietown, U.S.A.," *The Saturday Review of Literature,* XLVI (October 26, 1963). A mixed review of *Come on Out, Daddy.*

LEONARD, JOHN. "Whatever Happened to Bernard Wolfe?" *New York,* I (April 22, 1968). Devastating attack on *Move Up/ Dress Up/ Drink Up/ Burn Up* in contrast to Wolfe's earlier work.

MOON, BUCKLIN. "The Real Thing," *The New Republic,* CXV (November 4, 1946). Favorable review of *Really the Blues.*

MOORE, HARRY T. "Books in Brief," *The New Republic,* CXL (May 11, 1959). Short negative review of *The Great Prince Died.*

SCHULBERG, BUDD. "The Words Are Six Miles Tall," *Book Week* in *The New York Sunday Herald Tribune* (November 3, 1963). Mixed review of *Come on Out, Daddy.*

TALBOT, DANIEL. "Hippies and Beats," *The New York Times Book Review* (April 23, 1961). Extremely favorable review of *The Magic of Their Singing* and recognition of Wolfe's talent.

WOLFE, BERTRAM D. "Novel Based on Trotsky's Assassination," *The New York Herald Tribune Book Review* (March 29,

1959). Favorable review of *The Great Prince Died* as popularized history, with an attack on its psychological bent.

WYLIE, PHILIP. "After the Hydrogen Bombs," *The New York Herald Tribune Book Review* (December 14, 1952). An attack on the "outrageous" plot of *Limbo*.

Index

(The works of Bernard Wolfe are listed under his name)